19068

JN
515
.H25
1960

Haskins
    The growth of English
    representative government

THE GROWTH OF
ENGLISH REPRESENTATIVE GOVERNMENT

THE GROWTH OF ENGLISH

REPRESENTATIVE GOVERNMENT

Dy

GEORGE L. HASKINS

A PERPETUA BOOK

A. S. Barnes and Company, Inc.

New York

To
A. C. H.

CONTENTS

PREFACE

THE subject of this book is the growth of the English parliament from its beginnings in the thirteenth century to the outbreak of the civil wars in the seventeenth. So described the subject has been treated before, so that much of the material which is presented here will be familiar to those interested in parliamentary history. Recent investigations, however, have given historians cause to question the accepted outlines of even a generation ago, and it has accordingly seemed worth while to reëxamine the conclusions of earlier writers in the light of the sources and of recent studies. At the same time, the book is less concerned with describing the evolution of parliament in the period under discussion than with singling out the persistent currents in English society and government in order to show why the representative feature of parliament became its significant feature.

The substance of the book was delivered as a series of six lectures before the Lowell Institute of Boston in 1939. Two of the lectures were published in 1940 in *History* and in *Thought*,[1] but they have been entirely revised for inclusion in this book as Chapters I and II. Thanks are due to the Editors of those publications for permission to reprint that material in substantially the same form as that in which it first appeared. Chapter VI was published in 1947 in the *American Historical Review*[2] and is reprinted here with slight change through the kind permission of the Editor.

Much of the research and the writing which have gone into the book were done while I held an appointment in the So-

[1] "The King's High Court of Parliament Holden at Westminster," *History* (1940) xxiv. 295; "Counsel and Consent in the Thirteenth Century," *Thought* (1940) xv. 245.

[2] "Parliament in the Later Middle Ages," *American Historical Review* (1947) lii. 667.

ciety of Fellows at Harvard University, and I acknowledge with gratitude the opportunity which that appointment gave me to pursue the study of English constitutional history and law. The facilities for study and research afforded by the British Museum and the Harvard College Library are also acknowledged. Revision and rewriting have been aided by the efficient coöperation of the staff of the Biddle Law Library of the University of Pennsylvania in securing books for my use.

A book of this sort inevitably owes much to the work of other scholars in the field. To a considerable extent that obligation is reflected in the footnotes. Mere references, however, cannot express the debt which all students of parliamentary history owe to the detailed investigations of Mr. H. G. Richardson and Professor G. O. Sayles, and my own obligation to them I gratefully acknowledge. Several portions of the book, notably in Chapter IV, are based upon my researches in British archives, and I wish to thank the officials of the Public Record Office in London for their kindness and unfailing courtesy; of those officials, Mr. R. L. Atkinson has been especially helpful.

To the late President A. Lawrence Lowell I am particularly grateful for personal encouragement and for discussions which contributed greatly to my understanding of English government. I am also grateful to the late Professor Lawrence J. Henderson, of Harvard University, for suggestions and advice which were at all times helpful. I owe much to Professor Charles H. McIlwain, of Harvard University, under whose guidance I first undertook to study the history of parliament; and to Professor Sir Maurice Powicke and Mr. J. G. Edwards, of Oxford University, under whose direction I continued that work while a Henry Fellow at Merton College, Oxford.

Mr. Gaillard Lapsley, of Trinity College, Cambridge, has made several suggestions which I have adopted in Chapter II. My colleague Professor Francis S. Philbrick, of the University of Pennsylvania Law School, has given helpful advice with respect to the material in Chapter V. My step-daughter has shared the task of verifying references and through her care and exactitude has lightened the burden of preparing the manuscript for the press.

G. L. H.

Philadelphia,
October, 1947

THE KING'S HIGH COURT OF PARLIAMENT HOLDEN AT WESTMINSTER

DISSATISFACTION with representative institutions has of late become widespread. In continental Europe, the last two decades have witnessed the repudiation of those institutions in several countries. Elsewhere, particularly in England and the United States, there has been a growing conviction that representative government is not working well.[1] Among English writers several have urged that the parliamentary system is ill suited to conditions of the present century, that, because of its size, it operates too inefficiently for prompt and decisive action.[2] To many, as they look into the shadow of tomorrow, the vital question is whether representative institutions can be adapted to the needs of this century. No one can fail to note that the importance of the individual member of a representative assembly has declined with the extension of the governmental sphere. Modern problems, such as foreign affairs, currency, or agriculture, are sufficiently complicated to demand the attention of outside experts and technicians. Necessarily there is an increased reliance on the permanent civil service, and more and more power must be vested in the executive if the system is to function at all.

These tendencies are all symptoms of change and require many revaluations. Accordingly, it is not without interest to inquire into the beginnings of representative institutions, in order better to understand their nature. For the adequate

[1] For example, Ramsay Muir, *How Britain is Governed* (New York, 1930), pp. 3-9; George B. Galloway, *Congress at the Crossroads* (New York, 1946), p. 344: "Congress today is neither organized nor equipped effectively to perform its main functions of determining policy, reviewing executive performance, controlling expenditures, and representing the people."

[2] Compare H. J. Laski and others, *The Development of the Representative System in Our Times* (Lausanne, etc., 1928); Ramsay Muir, *Is Democracy a Failure?* (London, 1934); S. R. Daniels, *The Case For Electoral Reform* (London, 1938).

consideration of the functions of those institutions in modern society it is important to know how representative assemblies first came to be summoned, how they developed in societies of an earlier day, how they acquired their present-day characteristics. Too often, when an institution is studied, it is studied as an organism of independent development, important in itself, rather than as an artifice which contributes to the stability of the social equilibrium. Institutions must be studied as the language of an ever-changing society; indeed, as Thurman Arnold reminds us, we shall not be far wrong in thinking of the institutions of a society in much the same terms as those in which we think of its folklore.

The investigation of the origins of the English parliament has particular significance, for the modern world owes many of its political conceptions to England. Although representative assemblies were common features of the countries of western Europe in the Middle Ages, the English alone was not eclipsed—temporarily or otherwise—by the rise of the national monarchies in the fifteenth and sixteenth centuries. The British parliament has shown itself peculiarly adaptable to the many changes which have come about in the structure of English society. Indeed, even the monarchy of the Tudors enhanced its power, dignity, and authority. No less a prince than Henry VIII asserted in a speech to the house of commons, "We be informed by our judges that we at no time stand so highly in our estate royal as in the time of parliament, wherein we as head and you as members are conjoined and knit together in one body politic."[3] In the nineteenth century the British parliament, with the austerity of its traditions and its centuries of continuous existence, appeared to other nations a bulwark of liberty and a model of well-ordered government. New ideas about liberty and the sovereignty of the people, fostered by the French Revolution, bred an enthusiasm for representative institutions, typified by that of Eng-

[3] Quoted, A. F. Pollard, *The Evolution of Parliament* (London, 1920), p. 231.

land, which caused one nation after another to adopt some form of parliamentary government. In fact, all the parliamentary governments in Europe of the last hundred years were modeled, directly or indirectly, on the British parliaments. It has become a truism that England is the mother of parliaments.

Apart from such considerations of general interest, the actual workings of the English system as it stands today can be explained and understood adequately in terms only of what has gone before. The fusion of legislative, judicial, and executive functions in parliament, which is a peculiarity of the English constitution, is to be understood only from the fact that parliament evolved as a legislative assembly from a royal court of justice. The ceremonies today in the house of commons are largely medieval; and until 1872 the form of summons to members of parliament had run in the same words for six hundred years. The private bill, for example, as it is today, retains many characteristics of the medieval petition;[4] indeed, when in 1832 a committee was appointed for the reform of bill procedure, the members were instructed to investigate carefully the methods and records of medieval parliaments. Finally, attention should be drawn to one of the unique characteristics of the house of commons: that it is made up of delegates of self-governing, local communities which have become a permanent counterpoise to absolute political government.[5] The stability of representative government in England depends upon the stability of small, integrated local units—the town, the parish, and the county. The stability of a complex organization is always a direct function of the stability of the simple organization unit. This special situation in England is the outcome of a very long history of experience in self-government.

[4] T. E. May, *The Law, Privileges, Proceedings and Usage of Parliament* (14th ed., London, 1946), pp. 824-25.
[5] R. Gneist, *The History of the English Constitution* (New York, 1886), ii. 112, 358, note.

Most people, when they think of parliament or the house of commons, conjure up to the mind's eye the spectacle of the stately neo-Gothic Houses of Parliament on the Embankment of the Thames. But it is not with buildings such as these that the medieval parliament was associated, for they date only from the second quarter of the nineteenth century. Shadowed by those Houses, and by the towering Abbey of Westminster, lies the long bulk of gray-black stone known as Westminster Hall. No one edifice typifies so well the continuity of the English government; few places have been so intimately associated with its history. Its dark roof has rung with the acclamations that hailed many an heir to the throne; its somber flags have known the tread of throngs who sought to pay last homage to a sovereign king. It was here that the royal courts of justice had their first beginnings. Here the king's High Court of Parliament was convened; here, until the eighteenth century, the great trials for high treason were held. "The Great Hall of William Rufus," exclaims Macaulay in his famed description of the trial of Warren Hastings.[6] A great hall it is, and a masterpiece of early English architecture—in length all of two hundred and forty feet, in height nearly one hundred. In the proud boast of its builder, the Red King, son and heir of William the Conqueror, it was but a bedchamber in comparison with the building he intended to put up.[7]

Could we turn back the centuries in the glass of time, it would be a very different spectacle we should see at Westminster on a winter's morning in the opening years of the fourteenth century. No more the tapering pinnacles and crockets of neo-Gothic, nor the massive grays of Whitehall: instead, low-lying marshes and pasture land, flooded by a swollen Thames, sullenly resenting the massive walls and bulwarks of the royal palace on the Isle of Thorns. It is a wide and muddy Thames that runs with the salt tide by the palace, by

[6] T. B. Macaulay, "Warren Hastings," *Literary and Historical Essays* (Oxford, 1923), p. 618.

[7] J. Stow, *A Survey of the Cities of London and Westminster* (ed. Kingsford: Oxford, 1908), ii. 113.

the long staple of the woolmerchants, and by the gleaming white of the sumptuous Abbey church hard by. A slow river, with many a small fishing craft and much river traffic, running by the orchards of the Strand, past the river Fleet down to London City, with its red roofs, its lead-clad steeples, its hostels, its monasteries, its great cathedral church of St. Paul.

It is not to London City that we shall look on this early morning, but to the bustle and activity about the royal palace and the Great Hall at Westminster. It is Sunday, and the bells and chimes cannot be stilled; for King Edward I has returned from the North to consult with his magnates and the princes of the Church from all England, summoned by royal writ to attend his parliament at Westminster.

Edward, by the Grace of God, King of England, Lord of Ireland and Duke of Aquitaine, Greeting. Inasmuch as we wish to hold a special consultation with you and the other lords of this realm, touching certain establishments to be made concerning our land of Scotland, we strictly enjoin you, by the love and fidelity by which you are bound to us, and command that you shall put aside all other business and appear before us at our palace of Westminster on the Sunday after the Feast of St. Matthew the Apostle next ensuing, personally there to treat with us on these matters, in order that we may weigh your counsel.[8]

Parliament is a very solemn affair to which all the great of the kingdom must come. It is the great council of the realm, wherein appointments must be made, difficult cases discussed, and important matters of policy considered. For more than two hundred years now the kings of England have been following a practice, current throughout the kingdoms of Europe, of summoning to their courts at the great festivals of the Christian year their vassals, tenants-in-chief, and the princes of the Church, in order that they may hold "deep speech" with them. Yet the English kings are more than feudal lords. Of late, now, King Edward has stretched out his powerful administrative arm into the private feudal jurisdictions of the kingdom, questioning closely by what warrant

[8] Cf. *The Parliamentary Writs and Writs of Military Summons* (ed. Palgrave: London, 1827), i. 138.

they are held. His royal courts have multiplied, and his enemies declare that the land is wearied by excess of justice, by the constant questioning of royal justices, as they move from county to county, enquiring into the misdeeds of local officers and all manner of crime and malfeasance. King Edward is a powerful king, the "English Justinian" he will be called in time to come. He has opened his courts to the poorest and humblest subject, and step by step he is destroying local franchises and customs and building up a great body of uniform, national law. His parliament has thus become a great court of justice, wherein, as a contemporary lawyer describes it, "judicial doubts are determined, and new remedies are established for new wrongs, and justice is done to every one according to his deserts."[9] In his parliaments, held usually three times a year, the king is surrounded by lawyers from the courts, by jurists from the great Universities of Paris and Bologna, experts in the civil and canon law. Parliament is indeed a very solemn affair.

Besides counsel and justice, the king has found still another use for his parliaments. His elaborate administration requires many servants who must be paid; and he cannot give away his justice for nothing. His ordinary revenues do not suffice, for there is as yet no general taxation. He can ask a gracious aid from his barons and from the Church; but that again will not suffice. And so, following a precedent of recent years, writs have gone out to the sheriffs of every county in England, phrased in these words:

To the sheriff, greeting:
We firmly enjoin you to see to it that from your county two knights are elected without delay; and from each town or city in your county, two of the more discreet burgesses or citizens, capable of work. And they are to be made to appear before us at Westminster on the Sunday following the Feast of St. Matthew next ensuing. And these knights, citizens and burgesses are to have full and sufficient power for themselves and their respective communities to do and consent to those things which

9 *Fleta* (London, 1647), p. 66.

in our parliament shall be ordained, lest for lack of this power these matters should remain unaccomplished.[10]

It has become clear that there are many persons of property and wealth who are not actually among the magnates of the realm, particularly that there are many rich merchants in the towns and cities. And so two hundred of the townsfolk of England and seventy-four knights of the shire will respond to the summons; they have no choice. Altogether the numbers attending the king's parliament will be very nearly seven hundred: upwards of one hundred great prelates of the Church, one hundred and fifty representatives or proctors of the lower clergy, more than one hundred barons and earls, besides fifty or so of the king's official staff.

Such is the parliament the king has summoned. Of late it has been to the royal palace of Westminster that he has called his assembly, although there is no prescription by law or custom that he may not call it elsewhere. Although but a straggling village among the marshes, many sentiments of the people are crystallized about Westminster. Since before the coming of the Normans, it has been the recognized home of the king. The Conqueror was wont to hold his summer courts here, and for long the work of government and justice has centered about the royal palace. The pious Edward the Confessor, last of the Saxon kings, lived here and died here, and the Abbey church has in the course of time become the scene of royal coronations. "The crown, the grave, the palace, the festival . . . all illustrate the perpetuity of a national sentiment typifying the continuity of the national life."[11]

It is easy to understand that the summoning of a parliament means an enormous increase of activity about Westminster. Some days before this parliament was to meet, orders went out to the sheriffs of Surrey, Sussex, Kent, and London to purchase some three thousand bushels of wheat, much livestock, and over one hundred tuns of ale; wooden dishes,

10 Cf *Parliamentary Writs*, i. 115, 140.
11 W. Stubbs, *The Constitutional History of England* (Oxford, 1896), iii. 395.

brazen pots, and copper in mass were to be supplied.[12] There were to be many mouths to feed, for the king's household is large. And a week before, a grave and important-looking personage, called Master in Chancery, had stood forth in the Great Hall and silenced the noisy courts of law there assembled. Scroll in hand, he had read out his "crye," that the king was to gather his great council of the realm on the Sunday next ensuing. Continuing, he pronounced:

All who wish to bring forward petitions at this next parliament should deliver them day by day between now and the first Sunday in Lent, at the latest, to Sir John Kirkby, and Master John Bush, or to one of these. And they are assigned to receive them between now and the first Sunday in Lent.[13]

The same proclamation he had read publicly in the West Cheap, by St. Paul's in London, and also in the ancient Guildhall close by. And everywhere it had been greeted with applause, as the king thus proffered his readiness to hear any complaint. People had come to associate the relief of private grievances with the meeting of the king's parliament; and somewhere in their minds would echo the famed promise in the Great Charter of nearly a century ago, "to no one will we sell, to no one will we deny or delay right or justice."[14]

To others the holding of this parliament meant something very different. To most of the great tenants-in-chief, to most, that is, who were not perpetually attendant on the king's person, it meant a long and wearisome journey in the flood season from some remote corner of England, restless nights in smoke-clouded inns, with the dreary creaking of a loose blind outside, and the splash of rain in the mire-filled roads. It meant leaving the hunting, the comfort of the castle or the big manor house; it meant a dreary three weeks in London at one's own expense, with a wearying attention to details of

---

12 *Parliamentary Writs,* i. 407.
13 *Ibid.,* i. 155.
14 C. 40.

the king's affairs with Philip of France, or his dispute about the investiture of the new archbishop. The king would ask for money; and he would have new statutes to enact, currently described as amendments to the customary law, but in reality a fresh and insolent excuse to invade some local immunity or prerogative. Undoubtedly, the baron reflects, one of his own men will have the face to bring up some trifling case of injustice to the king's highest tribunal, and he, the lord, will be amerced or fined. The tedious journey to Westminster would entail little pleasure. Yet if he disobeys the summons, one of the ubiquitous royal officers will carry off a part of his goods until a fine has been paid.

To the lesser nobility, if we may use this term of the knights of the shire, the king's summons is equally irksome. Though closely connected by blood ties and other interests with the earls and barons, the elected knights are made to feel distinctly unimportant at the king's parliament. True, the knight senses he is vastly superior to the uncouth burgess representative from the town; and he has been elected to parliament because he is a prominent man in county affairs. The king may want official information as to the doings of royal officers, the bailiffs and sheriffs; the allegations of a petitioner may want corroboration. Unofficial testimony may be wanted, as to "what men are saying in remote parts of England, . . . and the possibilities of future taxation have to be considered."[15] None the less it is no privilege to come to Westminster, and the wages which his county will pay him, four shillings a day, will hardly balance his disbursements. He has had to find pledges, men who will guarantee his appearance in parliament, or perhaps four of his best oxen have been "bound over" by the sheriff, lest he try to escape the duty imposed by the king's summons.

Many of the elected knights have been before to the king's

[15] *Records of the Parliament Holden at Westminster, 1305* (ed. Maitland, Rolls Series: London, 1893), lxxv.

parliament.[16] They know what to expect. If, like John de Pabenham, knight of the shire for Bedford County in this parliament, there are any who were at the Michaelmas Parliament in 1297, they will recall the king's wrath when the knights and nobles in one body refused the king a grant of money until he had redressed their grievances about the forest laws.[17] Then, of an earlier day, one or two may recall that the knights and lords had promised the king a levy of a fifteenth on all their movable property, on condition that he would expel every Jew from England.[18] That was, they could reflect, a masterful stroke of genius. Oh yes, it was money the old king wanted, and when it had been promised he would bid them all go quietly and quickly, prepared to come again when they were needed. Why else had he thought to summon the vulgar townspeople, who spent their days dicing and drinking in an unsavory room at the Sign of the Rose, listening to vagrant student songs on an untuned lute?

After this fashion the baron or the knight might well be thinking as he crowds into the king's Great Hall beside the palace. Close on seven hundred persons are there, and the morning mists hang heavy about the old roof. Bay upon bay the stout chestnut of Normandy and the black oak of Ireland stretch on into the gloom to where at the end, surrounded by torches, sits King Edward I. His lined face and graying beard bear witness to relentless campaigns against the Scot and the turbulent Welsh, to ceaseless energies in building up his great administrative machine in the face of the tyranny of feudal franchises. Now he sits in his capacity as lawgiver, the English Justinian, holding his full court before the communities of the realm.

[16] Figures on the number of knights who were reëlected to Parliament at this time may be found in J. G. Edwards, "Personnel of the Commons in the Parliaments of Edward I and Edward II," *Essays in Medieval History Presented to T. F. Tout* (Manchester, 1925).

[17] *Chronicon Walteri de Hemingburgh* (ed. Hamilton: London, 1848-1849), ii. 148.

[18] *Annales Monastici* (ed. Luard, Rolls Series: London, 1866), iii. 362.

On his right is the Archbishop of Canterbury; on his left the Chancellor, William de Hamilton; below, some thirty members of the king's small council—his ministers and permanent official advisers. For reasons of comfort as well as in token of their dignity they sit upon great wool-sacks, brought in from the neighboring Woolstaple. Close at hand are the justices of the Common Pleas, the Exchequer, and the King's Bench; their advice will be needed during the session to frame any statutes the king may propose. Among them are the great lawyers of the day, Bereford and Ralph Hengham, whose learning and common sense have forged powerful links in the relentless chain of the king's justice.

Sitting apart are the ninety-five prelates of the realm, together with all manner of archdeacons and deans from the cathedral chapters. The king's business is not their business, they feel; even though they are ranked as an estate of the realm. But they know that if they do not attend parliament, in all likelihood there will be little left of their lands and property, which the barons and earls will almost certainly vote to tax. And at this moment there is grave fear that the king means to take action against the exporting of gold and other tribute to the Holy See in Rome.

Beyond stand the barons, earls, and other magnates of the realm, clothed in stamped velvets of blue, red, or yellow, with cloaks of silk and cloth of Tars. Their arms and weapons they have been forbidden to bear in time of parliament by an ordinance of the king, whose special peace, protecting all coming to parliament, he means to enforce.[19] It is not so long since the treasurer and other retainers of the Earl of Cornwall were murdered in the streets in broad daylight when on their way to parliament at Westminster.[20] And some can still remember how a jealous Archbishop of Canterbury set armed men upon the retainers of the Archbishop of York, broke his

---

[19] Cf. *Statutes of the Realm* (Record Commissioners: London, 1810), i. 170.
[20] *Calendar of the Patent Rolls, 1281-1292*, pp. 489, 517.

cross, and committed other outrages upon the prelate as he was making his way to parliament.[21]

Toward the back of the hall, mingled with the barons, are the knights of the shire, clad in velvet doublets, well lined with rich furs; and beyond, awkward and uncertain in a group of nearly two hundred, the citizens and burgesses elected by the towns. Two or three, like Gilbert de Rokesle, the great wool merchant and master of the exchange, seem to know their business and form the center of groups who talk about the grant of money that the king is sure to demand.

Suddenly the Bishop of London, clad in purple and scarlet, arises, and the talking ceases as he opens with a prayer. The Archbishop of Canterbury follows with a sermon on the text, "How shall a court correct the ills of the whole realm, unless it shall first be itself corrected." What is in store is now clear enough to many; and there are mutterings as the sermon comes to a close. How, they think, can the king reform his realm when his subjects in parliament are reluctant to grant him money? This is the plain meaning of what the Archbishop has been saying. Enough of this reform, it is in the mouths of many to cry. Let the king live of his own; let him mind his own affairs and leave other people alone to mind theirs. And many will instinctively pluck their purses from their sleeves and draw the strings together more closely.

Then silence again, as the Chancellor, the dignified Dean of York, William de Hamilton, addresses the assembled parliament. The purport of the summons to parliament is reiterated: the Archbishop, bishops, earls, barons, knights, and burgesses elected by the communities of the shires and towns have been called together in the king's parliament to discuss certain weighty affairs touching the safety of the realm and in particular the land of Scotland. The king wishes to urge that those who have petitions to present or grievances to be redressed are to bring their complaints to those of the king's

---

[21] *Historical Papers and Letters from the Northern Registers* (ed. Raine, Rolls Series: London, 1873), pp. 59-63.

council commissioned to receive them. Lastly he emphasizes that the king has incurred heavy expenses in connection with his wars, and especially because of the rebellion of Robert Bruce and others in the North. It is therefore of the utmost importance that the assembled communities should grant a gracious aid to the king for the better ordering of peace and quiet in the kingdom. He earnestly requests that the several estates should deliberate on the matter among themselves and report their decision to the council. Meanwhile, the hour being late—toward ten in the morning—the assembly is adjourned for the day.

The king, followed by his ministers and his council, leaves by the upper end of the hall into St. Stephen's Chapel; the clergy, the lay lords, and the knights remain to discuss the subsidy; the town representatives move off in disorderly groups across the Palace Yard and Dirty Lane toward the refectory of the Abbey, there to deliberate the share which they will grant the king. When these various orders have decided on the grant, as they will do very shortly, their work at the king's parliament is nearly ended.

It is, however, elsewhere than at the Great Hall that the main business of parliament will be accomplished; and it is by others than the great barons, the clergy, the elected knights and burgesses that that work will be done. Should we follow the day-by-day activities of the parliament after the opening of the session, it would be to the council chamber on the south side of the Old Palace Yard that we should repair.[22] Here we should soon understand that the king's parliament in the opening days of the fourteenth century is more in the nature of a high court of justice than a deliberative or legislative assembly. For it is the council, with the king as presiding officer, which is the heart and core of the medieval parliament—a council of ministers, judges, and experts in the law.

[22] In 1293 and in 1305 the council was assembled in the house of the Archbishop of York, which stood where the White Hall of later years was to stand. See *Rotuli Parliamentorum*, i. 91, 178.

In the great chamber beyond St. Stephen's Chapel, its roof thickly sown with golden stars on a background of azure, the council has its meeting place. In time to come this room will be known as the Star Chamber, and a mighty and powerful tribunal will take its name from the room. Now it is the center of all the work of consultation of a medieval parliament. Here, from early morning until nearly noon, the council will sit. Their work is confined to the early hours of the day, for, as Sir Henry Spelman shrewdly observes, "Our Ancestours and other the Northern Nations being more prone to distemper and excess of diet . . . used the Forenoon only, lest repletion [in food and drink] should bring upon them drowsiness and oppression of spirit. . . . To confess the truth, our Saxons were immeasurably given to drunkenness."[23]

Before the council knights of the shire will be called and appointed to administrative posts in their shires, and prominent burgesses will be summoned to find out what future customs can be imposed on the wool export. Before the council a deputation of prelates, barons, and knights will come at this parliament we have been describing to offer the king an aid of one-thirtieth to be assessed on their movable property. Before the council the burgesses will decide on a tax of one-twentieth to be levied on their goods. Finally, it is before the council that petitions for the redress of grievances will be presented, and before the council that the petitioner must appear, if he is wanted, to prosecute his case.

Before the representatives at this parliament return home, a group of townsfolk, representing their constituencies and perhaps feeling they should not return empty handed, will essay to make complaint that juries are corrupted by the rich and that ecclesiastical judges are meddling in temporal suits.[24] But the king and council will decide that the complaint has not sufficient foundation, and the petition will be dismissed. To this extent will the future house of commons attempt to

23 H. Spelman, *Posthumous Works* (Oxford, 1698), p. 89.
24 *Records of the Parliament of 1305*, p. 305, number 472.

participate in the king's parliament. It is not very difficult to see that the king and council are all-powerful, that the burgesses, even the knights of the shire, are no very essential part of parliament. There is something not a little ironical in the phrase of the summons which enjoins them to come to do what shall be ordained.

For when they have made their grant, when they have been given such instructions as the king sees fit, there will be another speech in the Great Hall to the assembled parliament of seven 'hundred. The king then addresses the estates in words preserved for us in a contemporary record:

Bishops and other prelates, counts, barons, knights of the counties, citizens and burgesses and other people of the community who have come to this parliament at the bidding of the lord king: greatly the king thanks you for your coming and wishes that you will return at once again to your home, so that you may come again quickly and without delay at whatever hour you shall be needed. But the bishops, counts, barons, judges, justices and other members of the lord king's council shall not go without special leave of the king. Those, too, who have business to transact before the council may remain and pursue their business.

And the knights of the shire who have come on behalf of the counties, and the others who have come on behalf of the cities and towns, are to go to Sir John Kirkby, who will make out writs for the payment of the expenses of their coming.[25]

The purpose for which the lesser barons, the elected knights and burgesses have been summoned is answered. The seventy councilors, together with their clerks and assistants, will remain; and the high court of parliament will still be considered in full session, even though the representatives and many magnates have gone home. It will remain in session for as much as three or four weeks, transacting the important business which has waited to come before the king's parliament.

There is much business. Nicholas Segrave has been accused of high treason in the Scottish campaign and must be in-

25 *Parliamentary Writs*, i. 155.

dicted before the king in council. Now that the war is over, a settled form of government must be provided for Scotland—a task that will demand long debates. The Bishop of Glasgow, the Earl of Carrick, and John Mowbray will be called before the council to say how Scotland should be represented at the king's Midsummer parliament in the same year.[26] There will be discussion of policy to be pursued in the lately recovered province of Aquitaine; vast quantities of writs will have to be issued for payments in arrears, and there will be important appointments to be made there, from the seneschal downwards.[27]

The greatest activity of the king and council involves the despatching of hundreds of petitions which have come in from all over the kingdom, as well as from Scotland, Ireland, and Gascony. Four-fifths of the records which this parliament will leave behind are concerned with those petitions and the action consequent upon them. Committees will have been appointed to deal with them, and no suitor will be turned away. The citizens of Lincoln will protest against the abuse of a local franchise in prejudice to their rights.[28] The University of Cambridge will ask leave to found a college.[29] The citizens of Norwich will ask for the grant of a special aid for murage for the safety of the city.[30] Simon le Parker will plead by petition that he has not received justice before the king's judges and is being held on suspicion of murder in the gaol at Canterbury.[31]

Oftentimes the courts of common law, even though sufficiently honest, were not sufficiently strong to do justice in cases where a powerful magnate interfered. The power of granting relief lay in the king, and extraordinary jurisdiction could be, and was, exerted in behalf of an otherwise helpless

[26] *Records of the Parliament of 1305*, pp. 14-16.
[27] *Ibid.*, pp. 328-38.
[28] *Ibid.*, pp. 305-6, number 473.
[29] *Ibid.*, p. 33, number 50.
[30] *Ibid.*, pp. 48-49, number 78.
[31] *Ibid.*, p. 11, number 10.

suitor.[32] And so the idea of relief of private grievances fast became an essential characteristic of the king's parliament. It came to be a court placed over all other courts, for the purpose, as the contemporary lawyer reminds us, of resolving doubtful judgments, providing new remedial measures for newly emergent wrongs and meting out justice to all according to their deserving.[33]

As early as the eighth year of Edward I's reign, we hear that the multitude of petitions presented in parliament have been giving a good deal of trouble. An order in 1280 declares that "the folk who come to the king's parliament are often delayed and disturbed to the great grievance of them and of the court by the numerous petitions which are presented to the king."[34] It is therefore provided that there shall be official triers of petitions, who will sort them out. Only those "which are so great or of so much grace" that they cannot otherwise be dealt with are to come before the king himself.[35]

Actually, the response which a petition received seldom gave the suppliant what he asked for. In Maitland's words, "he was merely put in the way of getting it."[36] The council, says Sir Matthew Hale, "rarely (if at all) exercised any decision or decisive jurisdiction upon them, but only a kind of deliberative power."[37] The council transmitted them to those persons or courts which had properly cognizance of the causes. The field of government discretion is wide, yet many petitions are easily settled.

Probably there would be an outcry if the religious houses could not pretty easily obtain licences for the acquisition of a reasonable quantity of land; if the nobleman who is going abroad were not suffered to appoint a general attorney; if the burghers of this or that town could not without much difficulty get leave to tax themselves and their

---

[32] *The Collected Historical Works of Sir Francis Palgrave* (ed. Thompson: Cambridge, 1922), viii, 114.
[33] Above, note 9.
[34] Quoted, *Records of the Parliament of 1305*, p. lvi.
[35] *Ibid.*
[36] *Ibid.*, p. lxviii.
[37] M. Hale, *The Jurisdiction of the Lords House* (London, 1796), p. 67.

neighbours by way of murage, pontage, or pavage; still in any particular case the request may be refused and no reason given for the refusal.[38]

If the description of a session of the king's high court of parliament holden at Westminster in the opening years of the fourteenth century has seemed over-long, it is because the picture is not so simple as might be supposed. Many of the records are scattered, and even at best they are few. As we look back through the vista of six centuries, we can see that there is much that is unfamiliar. Today we know that the English parliament stands above the king. It is hard to visualize a time when parliament was the instrument of a very powerful king, when the men who attended it came because they had to and thought attendance no privilege. Nothing is more difficult than to think away the distinctions of a later age, "distinctions which seem to us as clear as sunshine."[39] Nothing, as Sir Henry Spelman observes, is more common than for succeeding ages to view "what is past by the present, conceive the former to have been like to that they live in, and framing thereupon erroneous propositions, to likewise make thereon erroneous inferences and Conclusions."[40]

It is perhaps not unnatural for people to expect to discover in the medieval parliaments the essential traits in embryo which characterize parliament of today. We shall hardly, of course, expect to find a system of ministerial responsibility and an elaborate party machine, any more than we shall imagine the Venerable Bede correcting proof-sheets for the press. Yet it has probably perplexed many not to have found, in the description given, something that can be more clearly identified as the house of commons, something else that bears the earmarks of the house of lords or the privy council. Many textbooks and reputable histories still tell how

[38] *Records of the Parliament of 1305*, p. lxviii.
[39] F. W. Maitland, *Township and Borough* (Cambridge, 1898), p. 11.
[40] H. Spelman, *Posthumous Works*, p. 57.

Edward I created in 1295 a parliamentary model for all time, how he enfranchised the third estate and laid the foundations of the house of commons. But as we look at the records of the medieval parliaments, we are led to question the truth of such assertions.

We are struck first of all by the small part played by the so-called enfranchised class, the elected representatives from the counties and towns. We are struck, too, by their entire lack of organization. Above all we see that, unlike today, parliament cannot be equated with the house of commons. The business of the session is not initiated by the knights and burgesses. No legislation is framed on bills presented by them: indeed, they are not even consulted on any proposed changes in the law. We see that those representatives hold the purse strings; yet they make little attempt to exercise any control over policy. Finally, we note that the greater number of those who attend the parliament do so under compulsion and consider it an altogether unpleasant duty.

On the other hand is the curious feature to which attention has been drawn: the main work of the session is performed by the king and his council. The core and essence of the medieval parliament is a session of this council of permanent official advisers, the judges and justices, the important earls, the great prelates of the realm. They are responsible for framing statutes, answering petitions, listening to cases on appeal, and otherwise attending to the multifarious details of the government of the kingdom. It is all too apparent—in spite of those who would have us see in the medieval parliament a struggling but politically self-conscious house of commons—that the representative knights and burgesses, with their shifting personnel, are as yet no integral or even essential part of parliament. They have little share in the work of government.

For all this we can recognize, even at first glance, practices from which the parliament of today will derive. Knights of the shire and burgesses from the boroughs and towns are elected by constituencies for which they act as representative delegates to a central assembly. Taxes are levied with the consent of these representatives, who come to the king's parliament with full power to bind their constituencies. Moreover, the caliber of the representatives is reasonably high. For one thing, they are chosen from among the more discreet and capable men; for another, they have had considerable experience in local government—the knights of the shire in judicial and administrative posts in the counties, the burgesses in dealing with the affairs of gilds and large municipal communities. So much we can see of parliament and the beginnings of representative government in the opening years of the fourteenth century.

The most persistent phenomena, it has been observed, are on the whole the most important. The temperature of the blood, for example, is a constant to which all physicians attach the highest importance. This observation is no less true of human institutions than of the human body. The use of representation is a political phenomenon which has been associated with the operation of the English government for six or seven hundred years. The particular institution with which it has been associated is parliament. In the course of those centuries the complexion, even the structure of parliament, has changed radically; but from the end of the thirteenth century the use of elected representatives in parliament has been constant. In the course of time this practice has become a basic fact in modern political institutions. For those reasons, it is useful to seek to understand the nature of parliamentary assemblies in the Middle Ages.

2

COUNSEL AND CONSENT IN THE THIRTEENTH CENTURY

THE description given in the preceding chapter of a typical session of a parliament at the beginning of the fourteenth century revealed that the session was dominated by the king and by the experts of his council. It indicated that the part played in the session by most of the great magnates who were summoned, and by the elected representatives, was slight. It further appeared that the business of a parliament was largely judicial and administrative, concerned with providing new legal remedies where the existing law was inadequate or where the judgment of an inferior court had failed. Parliament, in other words, appeared rather to be a court of justice than a legislative assembly.

It is true that at a meeting of parliament a certain amount of other business might be transacted. Officials would be asked to give account of their stewardships; there might be some consultation and deliberation among the magnates and the officials of the council; very likely the barons and the representatives of the counties and towns would be asked to help the king out of financial straits by the grant of an aid. But when all is said and done, parliament was the time and the place for petitioning for favors and for remedying wrongs. When every nonessential has been stripped away, the essence of parliaments "is the dispensing of justice by the king or by someone who in a very special sense represents the king."[1]

In the fourteenth century there is one thing, then, that the word "parliament" does not mean: "parliament" does not mean "house of commons." There was no house of commons. It is all too easy to attach a modern significance to a word

[1] H. G. Richardson and G. O. Sayles, *Bulletin of the Institute of Historical Research* (1928), v. 133.

which we meet in the records of many centuries ago. In the early 1300's the word "parliament"—or, in the French vernacular of the day, *parlement*—is by no means new. It is found as early as the eleventh century in the *Chanson de Roland*.[2] Originally it meant a "talking-together," a "colloquium." The chronicler Joinville tells us how, in order to escape the jealous eye of Queen Blanche, Louis IX and his wife used to meet secretly together on the back stairs of the palace and "hold their parliament."[3] But by the end of the thirteenth century in England, the word is being used more and more to apply to solemn assemblies or courts summoned by the king—assemblies at which the great laymen and ecclesiastics of the realm are present, and also elected representatives from the counties and towns of all England. What distinguishes these assemblies called "parliament" from others which are variously called *tractatus*, or *colloquia*, is the hearing of petitions for legal redress. "The 'parleying' from which they took their name was primarily legal."[4]

The predominantly judicial (as opposed to legislative) character of those early assemblies, both in England and in France, has been established beyond much question. The English parliament, like the *parlement* of Paris, was primarily a court set over other courts; the business of such assemblies was what we should call judicial and administrative.[5] However, insistence on a particular function or aspect of an institution, no matter how "operational" its significance, can easily obscure the real character of the institution and its importance in the society within which it functions. Because matters of law and administration bulk large, the official records which have come down to us tend to give an impersonal idea of the early parliaments. There is the risk that the

2 *La Chanson de Roland* (ed. Bédier: Paris, 1924), p. 214.
3 *Histoire de Saint Louis* (ed. de Wailly: Paris, 1874), p. 332.
4 J. E. A. Jolliffe, *The Constitutional History of Medieval England* (New York, 1937), p. 340.
5 On the affinities between parliament and the *parlement* of Paris see H. G. Richardson, "The Origins of Parliament," *Transactions of the Royal Historical Society*, 4th ser. (1928) xi. 137.

early assemblies may be looked upon as a mere chapter in medieval administrative history. We dare not say, writes Professor Powicke, that the growth of parliament "was inevitable or impersonal, and divorce it from the convictions of ordinary men and women, for these convictions gave it life."[6] There are, in other words, other factors besides judicial and administrative convenience, or the royal need for money, to explain the calling of the first representative assemblies in England. It is the purpose of this chapter to point to certain of those factors and to trace their significance in the early development of parliament.

To a century like the last one, accustomed to progress and to the social changes that it was thought could be effected by conscious effort, it seemed entirely plausible that a democratically minded Simon de Montfort should devise a scheme for including representatives of the nation in the king's councils. To a generation accustomed to see boards and institutions set up or created by Act of Parliament, it seemed entirely plausible that a constitutionally minded Edward I should carry on the work of Earl Simon and should create the house of commons. Voltaire's epigram that history is a pack of tricks which we play upon the dead was often exemplified in the glowing accounts of parliament written in the nineteenth century. If it is the truth which is to be sought, the myths of Simon de Montfort's parliament in 1265 and Edward's Model Parliament of 1295 must be dismissed along with such legends as the landing of the Pilgrims on Plymouth Rock. For myths of that sort there is no foundation of fact. The origins of parliament and of representative government are to be found not in any deliberate act of creation, but in the social fabric of the age. They are to be found in the practice of feudal kings who summoned their vassals to their

[6] F. M. Powicke, in *Harvard Tercentenary Publications: Independence, Convergence, and Borrowing in Institutions, Thought, and Art* (Cambridge. Mass., 1937), p. 145.

courts on stated festivals of the Christian year, there to deliberate and take counsel on the weighty affairs of the kingdom.

Most people who consider thoughtfully the evidence of history will perceive that the changes and developments in institutions were seldom contemplated by the people who brought them about. As President Lowell has written in a suggestive essay, the steps people took "were consciously and rationally taken to meet certain immediate needs without a thought of possible ultimate consequences."[7] The barons of 1215 who wrested the Great Charter from King John had no idea that they were establishing the right to trial by peers. The men who sought to retain the great offices of state in the time of Queen Anne through control of a majority in the house of commons little thought that they were establishing the foundations of what we now call the Cabinet system. The case is much the same with the beginnings of parliament. Parliament grew out of what we loosely call the "feudal system," the handiwork not of democratic initiative, but of autocratic kings who sought to strengthen their own power.

It is a not uncommon misconception that the feudal system was a form of government midway between aristocracy and tyranny, whereby the peasants and small land-owners were exploited in the interests of a landed nobility. Many people have come to believe that this government was "inefficient, corrupt, and tyrannical, and that its agents were greedy, venal, cruel, and disloyal."[8] Occasionally modern writers can be found who point to feudalism as a hideous parallel to present-day "economic royalism" and its relentless hold over oppressed minorities.

Contemporary official records tell a different story, however, and suggest that, far more than some may like to realize, the feudal system secured countless mutual advantages and services to both lord and vassal and involved from the start

---

[7] A. Lawrence Lowell, *What a University President Has Learned* (New York, 1938), p. 137.

[8] R. F. Treharne, *The Baronial Plan of Reform, 1258-1263* (Manchester, 1932), p. 37.

mutual consent. Many of the English private charters of the twelfth century give us glimpses of groups of barons advising a great tenant-in-chief, or approving what he has done.[9] The baronial courts "advised their lords in the crises which continually arose in the history of every great fee, and thereby evolved in course of time a coherent scheme of rights and duties out of the tangle of personal relationships."[10] It has been observed that in these feudal courts "the determination to reconcile order and justice, to find some working compromise between English and Normal customs . . . produced a working system in which both authority and responsibility were distributed between lord and man, and not concentrated solely in the superior to whom deference and loyalty were owed by the inferior."[11] Sentiments of loyalty and responsibility there were on both sides, mingled with such important ideas as respect for an established order, sanctioned by the habits of their forefathers and a universal Christian church. The powerful English kings set their faces against the centrifugal forces which feudalism could so easily breed, and stood out for coöperation between the orders of society, for counsel and consent.

Long before the Norman William landed on English shores, the Saxon kings had been wont to call about them on stated occasions the great of the land in church and state. Office or personal tie was the basis of membership in these national assemblies, which were known as the council of wise men, the witanagemot. With the consent of the witan the king published his laws and decided on weighty matters of policy affecting the peace of the kingdom. Taxation and the affairs of the Church were considered within the competence of this assembly, and before it, as a tribunal of last resort, the king judged appeals on important civil and criminal causes.

---

[9] Cf. W. Dugdale, *Monasticon Anglicanum* (London, 1849), v. 26: "cum consilio et assensu baronum et hominum nostrorum."

[10] F. M. Stenton, *The First Century of English Feudalism* (Oxford, 1932), p. 44.

[11] H. M. Cam, *Liberties and Communities of Medieval England* (Cambridge, 1944), pp. xii-xiii.

After the Conquest, the Norman and Plantagenet kings built on Anglo-Saxon foundations. To secure the adhesion of the conquered kingdom, they stressed the continuity of the Saxon and Norman rule. Thus the laws and customs prevailing under Edward the Confessor were to continue in full force; the structure of local government—centered in the courts of the shire and the hundred—was to remain unaltered. If the feudalism of the Continent was introduced, it was to strengthen and invigorate ancient institutions with the adventurous and highly strung energy of the Norman rulers. Such changes as there were took the form of increased supervision by royal authority. Thus the national military levy of an earlier day was transformed into the feudal levy, for land was henceforth to be held on condition of military service. Again, the local independence that had belonged to the Saxon earls was curbed, although their administrative functions in local affairs was continued. The idea of a general council, too, was perpetuated; and although the complexion of the witanagemot was changed, and although some of its competence was diminished because of the greater power of the king, the feudal council continued to advise the king as before on important decisions and in difficult judicial cases.

England under the Norman kings was "a small, well-conquered kingdom,"[12] and it was ruled as forcefully and as personally as any baron ruled his own manor. England and the fullness thereof was the king's, and though a kingdom it was regarded as the king's private fief. There was, in effect, no law of kingship as such (despite the existence of considerable political writing about it), for the king's rights were regarded simply as intensified private rights because he was the most powerful person. To his fief, as to the lesser lordships of any baron, were attached all the rights and jurisdictions incident to feudal tenure. By a custom introduced from Normandy, a lord was entitled to demand of his vassals what was broadly called "aid" and "counsel." By the same custom,

12 F. W. Maitland, *Law Quarterly Review* (1898), xiv. 33.

the king was entitled to demand them from his tenants-in-chief. "Aid" meant military service in the feudal levy. "Counsel" meant periodic suit at court, to give advice on questions of law and custom and to participate in the adjustment of right and procedure between individuals. Counsel, so far as it concerned the king's court, involved to a great extent the principal functions of the old witanagemot, with this difference, that the Norman kings made attendance compulsory. Dicey put it very well when he said, "It was rather the King's privilege than his duty to receive counsel."[13]

Insistence on suit at court, as an incident of feudal service, was of first importance because it operated as a force which helped to unify the baronage and hence successfully combatted the centrifugal forces of feudalism. In contemporary France, the king was not strong enough to demand of the nobility regular and periodic suit at court. In consequence, France broke up into the great dynastic feudatories which lasted throughout the Middle Ages. In England, because the king was strong enough to enforce his will, that result did not occur. The possible ill effects of the "clannishness of the shires" and the pertinacious local distinctions and rivalries were avoided by the Norman policy.

At the same time, it must be remembered that the English kings of the twelfth and thirteenth centuries were more than feudal lords. They ruled also as national sovereigns. Their handiwork stands out increasingly at every point in the administration, for they were great builders. Private baronial jurisdictions were undermined by the establishment of new royal courts, new forms of action, new possessory assizes for the recovery of land. Royal justices itinerant traveled about England, trying cases and building up the king's power. Slowly, very slowly, the strength of the royal power became felt in every corner of England; the feudal regime was placed on a national basis.

As much as any other single fact, the king's insistence on

[13] A. V. Dicey, *The Privy Council* (London, 1887), p. 3.

the feudal obligation of suit at court was responsible for the extension all over England of an administration which was national as well as royal. The regular appearance of the tenants-in-chief at the king's court assured the king a hand in supervising the local jurisdictions of his barons, and in extending the common law at the expense of local custom. Those appearances were both tedious and objectionable, for in speaking of attendance at any medieval court we must always put duty before right. None the less, the result was a kind of political education. In the same way, the participation of the various earls in the life and administration of the great honours had developed in them a sense of responsibility to community life.[14] Now, under pressure from above, they became accustomed to coöperation in the work of royal government. It is hardly going too far to say that the obligation of suit at the king's court became, in the thirteenth century, the framework upon which the structure of parliament was reared.

The process by which the feudal administration was nationalized and by which the baronage of England was educated to a sense of responsibility in the establishment of law and in the adjustment of rights between groups and individuals was not accomplished all at once or without opposition. Three significant stages may be observed in the process. The first, during the reign of Henry II, witnessed a more or less constant state of friction between the king and the barons, in which the king did his utmost to wipe out independent baronial franchises and jurisdictions which hampered the extension of royal power. The policy was in the main successful, and in passing to the second stage we can see that a degree of coöperation was attained between the rivals which may fairly be described as a state of equilibrium; as a prominent feature of the thirteenth century, it should occupy much of our attention. At the third stage, the equilibrium has broken down; and in the struggle to reëstablish it, there is

---

14 Cf. Stenton, *First Century of English Feudalism*, p. 94.

raised the whole question of the basis of authority in the state. It will be useful to ask how that equilibrium was thrown out of balance and what measures were taken to deal with the problems created.

In the twelfth century, the crowning boast of a baron could be, "If I do you wrong, who is there to do you right?"[15] The credit of bringing to nought the implications of so proud an assertion of independence belongs to Henry II. Case after case his writs drew into the new royal courts, as circuit justices traveled about the kingdom trying men for every manner of crime. Royal officials, sheriffs, bailiffs, guardians of the forest were everywhere, reporting breaches of the peace, and supervising the doings of men all over England. Link by link the relentless chain of uniform law was forged out of the very stuff that sought to break it asunder; and step by step the common law was built up, that is to say, a law common to all England.

For a long time, of course—well after the reign of Henry II —local jurisdictions and privileges continued in private hands and were jealously guarded by their holders. Every new royal encroachment was resisted as strenuously as are the extensions of federal authority in this country today. The introduction of new institutions, such as the jury and circuit justices, was in fact opposed as vehemently as the recent proposals for the reorganization of the Supreme Court of the United States— and on many of the same grounds.

However, neophobia is a temporary illness, and people soon observed that the new forms of action which could be pleaded in the royal courts were useful and advantageous in the recovery of land wrongly taken or withheld. People saw that the presentment jury of twelve men was a serious deterrent to crime and violence. They saw, moreover, that royal justice was more speedy than baronial justice, and that the

15 *Matthaei Parisiensis Chronica Majora* (ed. Luard, Rolls Series: London, 1880), v. 738.

new methods of proof by witnesses, instead of by the anti-
quated ordeal, were far more certain than the old.

While the king was attempting to absorb baronial jurisdictions by extending the sphere of royal administration, the
baronage was being forced to coöperate with the king to help
achieve his ends. Judges, sheriffs, and other royal officials were
recruited largely from the baronage, and a sense of responsibility wider than the manor or the fief was inevitably fostered. The new actions at law, the extension of a common
system, helped to breed something of a common point of
view in widely separated districts of the kingdom. Finally,
the obligation of suit at court meant that the officials and
the tenants-in-chief met together on a common ground with
common problems in the king's council. It was natural that
some corporate feeling should develop. In time the enlarged
council came to exercise a measure of control over the king.

No king, neither Henry II, nor Richard, nor John, was
conscious of what was really happening; none of them was
responsible for any direction toward effecting this coöperation. On the contrary, each aimed simply and solely at extending the royal power and at an effective royal administration. The end attained, a limited rather than an absolute
monarchy, was entirely different from the one they had in
view.

In the writings of Bracton we find the statement: "The
king has his councilors who are his associates; he who has
associates has a master."[16] This sentence illustrates something
of the development of baronial counsel in the twelfth and
thirteenth centuries. As early as the reign of Henry I, it is
recorded that a new law or edict which changes custom must
have the common consent of the barons of the kingdom if it

[16] Bracton, *De Legibus et Consuetudinibus Angliae* (ed. Woodbine: New
Haven, 1915 ff.), ii. 110. Probably this is not Bracton's own statement, but it
makes its appearance in the manuscripts of his work very shortly after his
death and may be taken to indicate current views as to the nature of the king's
council. For technical criticism on the appearance of this *addicio* in the manuscripts, see *ibid.*, i. 252, 322-33; F. W. Maitland, *Bracton's Note Book* (London,
1887), i. 29-33; G. Lapsley, *History* (1938), xxiii. 9-10.

is to be binding beyond the king's lifetime.[17] Henry II's famous Assize of Clarendon and his Assize of the Forest were established with the counsel and consent of the bishops, barons, counts, and nobles of the realm.[18] A century or so later, Bracton says that whatever has been defined or approved by the counsel and consent of the magnates has, on the authority of the king, the force of law.[19]

What happened was this. By compelling the barons to coöperate in the work of government and accept certain definite responsibilities, the king sponsored the growth of the council as an institution. It became something quite different from the vague, general assemblies of the witanagemot. Concurrently, the feeling grew that matters affecting the interest of the king's subjects must be done with their approval. Counsel, in other words, came to involve consent. The realm is still regarded as the king's private fief; the law administered is his law, the feudal law of the fief. Nevertheless the king is felt to have a clear responsibility to his subjects with regard to changes or innovations in the law. Above all, the rule is established in the never-to-be-forgotten words of the Great Charter: "No scutage or aid, save the customary feudal ones, shall be levied except by the common counsel of the realm."[20]

In connection with the enlarging functions of the king's council, a significant principle of political action was worked out, namely, the principle of majority rule.[21] In the course of the growth of parliament, that principle became a matter of great importance. But like many other characteristics of parliament, it was something that was first worked out in the feudal council, long before representatives of the commons

[17] M. M. Bigelow, *Placita Anglo-Normannica* (London 1879), p. 145. The case is discussed further by G. B. Adams, *Council and Courts in Anglo-Norman England* (New Haven, 1926), p. 118.
[18] W. Stubbs, *Select Charters Illustrative of English History* (ed. Davis: Oxford, 1913), pp. 170, 186.
[19] Bracton, *De Legibus* (ed. Woodbine), ii. 19.
[20] C. 12.
[21] For a recent discussion of the principle of majority rule, see S. B. Chrimes, *English Constitutional Ideas in the Fifteenth Century* (Cambridge, 1936), pp. 133-37.

were added. The principle is traceable in some degree to the influence of Roman law and the practice of the ecclesiastical courts. In the secular courts in England, from the moment the records first begin, there appears a strong desire for unanimity. In early times, the judgment of a court was regarded in a very real sense as the judgment of the whole district within which the court was held. It took some time for men to accept the dogma that the voice of the majority was the voice of the community. People felt that the community, like a corporation, could have only one voice. The principle of unanimity was inherited by the jury, and survives of course today as one of the first conditions of the jury's verdict.

But as the function of speaking for the community devolved more and more upon the jury, the feeling grew in the courts that in case of a disagreement the opinion of the majority was to prevail. Instances of this notion occur as early as the so-called *Laws of Henry I.*[22] Whether the notion is attributable to the ideas of an aristocratic society, wherein the powerful thegn was regarded as "better" than any one of his vassals, it is difficult to say. It is plain, however, that early in the twelfth century the practice of following the voice of the majority became more prevalent in secular courts and councils. The acceptance of the practice is certainly connected with the development of Canon law and the revival of Roman law. The Church introduced the idea of the "larger and wiser part," the *maior et sanior pars,* as a fundamental principle of corporate decision. The canonists linked that idea to the Roman doctrine of coercion in majority rule through the very convenient fiction that the act of the majority raised a presumption of greater wisdom, of *sanioritas.*[23]

In 1215 the barons proposed that the twenty-five of their number who were to enforce their articles on King John

---

[22] *Leges Henrici Primi,* v. 6: "Quodsi in iudicio inter partes oriatur dissensio, de quibus certamen emerserit, uincat sententia plurimorum." F. Liebermann, *Die Gesetze der Angelsachsen* (Halle, 1903), i. 549.

[23] O. Gierke, *Das Deutsche Genossenschaftsrecht* (Berlin, 1868 ff.), iii. 322 ff.

should proceed, in case of disagreement, by vote of the majority.[24] The proposal was actually incorporated in the final clause of Magna Carta, where it is established: "Let that be considered valid and firm which the greater part of those who are present arrange or command, just as if the whole twenty-five had agreed in this."[25] The practice thenceforward enjoyed considerable publicity. In the Provisions of Oxford, in 1258, the principle is clearly laid down as the rule for the king's council.[26]

The idea that the majority could bind the dissenting minority helped naturally to form a theory of the corporateness of the council. It helped to give the council status as a definite institution which had real political power, for it meant that nothing could be gained by the baron who retired from deliberations and sulked in his castle. If it was a scutage or an aid to which the majority had consented, the recalcitrant baron would be forced to pay the tax whether he liked it or not. Hence it was no great step to the assumption that those barons present at a meeting of the council could act for and bind those who were absent. A very significant stage had been reached in the development of the baronage as a corporate and politically self-conscious power whose counsel and consent potentially meant more than the privilege of simply approving the king's acts.

Other factors, however, are of as great significance in the development of counsel and consent. The political events in the opening years of the thirteenth century have in general obscured the importance of the reign of John. His quarrel with the king of France, culminating in the loss of half the English possessions on French soil; the Interdict, and the consequent surrender of the kingdom to the Pope; the wars and excessive taxation; finally, the revolt of the barons, crowned by the settlement in that famous treaty, the Great Charter,

24 Stubbs, *Select Charters*, p. 291.
25 *Ibid.*, p. 302.
26 *Ibid.*, p. 381.

in 1215—these events are writ large across the pages of our histories. They divert attention from the organic developments of society.

Seldom can a single event be said radically to influence the subsequent course of history. However, in 1205 King John forfeited the duchy of Normandy to Philip Augustus. This event seems to have had an immediate result in unifying the barons in England. Those who held lands in both England and France were obliged to choose to which king they would owe their allegiance. The barons who were prepared to sacrifice their French lands no longer had a divided allegiance, and they were free for the first time to devote themselves exclusively to English affairs. Professor Powicke has observed that thereafter public men were "not so distracted as their predecessors had been by the association of England with other large and important fiefs."[27] Political reflection becomes more constant and more purposeful.

It is in the reign of John that we first meet with a word which describes the barons as a class, rather than as individuals. The word *baronagium* makes its appearance. John himself, as we can see from his charters and other diplomatic instruments, was the first king regularly to style himself "king of England" rather than "king of the English." Some sense of nationalism is clearly forming, as commerce increases and breaks down local self-sufficiency. We can see it in the demands of the townsfolk for uniform customs and trade regulations, a coherent system of weights and measures. It is in the reign of John that we first hear of an "English" church. In short, "through a process that is obscure in the extreme, but a process in which the decline of chivalry, the growth of the new learning, the increasing size of the known world . . . must have played a great part,"[28] we begin to see the emergence of an England where the loyalty to a class is broadening out into a sense of national solidarity.

27 Powicke, *Harvard Tercentenary Publications,* p. 138. Cf. also his *Loss of Normandy* (Manchester, 1913), pp. 411 ff.
28 C. H. McIlwain, *The High Court of Parliament* (New Haven, 1910), p. 52.

It has been suggested that England in the thirteenth century "lived as she lived in the reigns of Elizabeth and Victoria," that men were "conscious of some form of general will which could be expressed by the whole body of responsible men summoned together to discuss the affairs of the realm—the body described as the 'communitas regni.' "[29] It was an era of peace and prosperity, when men felt confident in the existing social order.

The generation which came to manhood in the opening year of the thirteenth century had lived through a time of great experiences. Its spirit had been nourished on the new literature, science, and discovery of the great Latin renaissance of the twelfth century. Its eyes, in the words of Professor Powicke,

had rejoiced in new forms of art, a marvellous activity in the building of churches, monasteries, castles, bridges, whose austerity was consistent with the reception of new devices or luxuries. Some of these young nobles had brought back from the East ineffaceable memories of a crusade under the greatest leader of his time [Richard the Lion-Hearted]. . . . They had seen Château Gaillard rise with the rapidity of a miracle and had heard the bitter news of its capture. . . . They had learned that the new administrative system could be as interesting as a tournament, and was far more closely related to the problems presented in the management of their own estates. The experience of all had impressed upon them the duty of loyalty. . . . Whether they continued to cling to the king or not, the more serious men among the baronage must have learned to interpret the traditions of personal loyalty and the feudal contract in a larger way. . . . Beneath all the violence and impulsiveness of society in this time, the hatred of some, the lethargy or selfishness of others, we can feel at work the impulse to a new adventure in response to the idea that administration is a public, not merely a personal, task.[30]

Coherence as well as cohesion was given to this new outlook of society by an influence we can never, in speaking of the Middle Ages, forget for a moment. I mean the Roman Catholic Church. The most powerful social and intellectual force

29 Powicke, *Harvard Tercentenary Publications*, pp. 135, 143.
30 *Cambridge Medieval History* (Cambridge, 1929), vi. 219.

in western Europe in the Middle Ages, it is difficult for people today to realize the dominance of the Church over the minds and habits of men. Not even the radio or modern journalism can match the influence of the parish priest, who, week after week, century after century, told and retold the story whose theme swept the whole path of history—"the story of a chosen people, of divine governance from creation to the founding of their own church, guarded in a sacred book and interpreted from a sacred tongue."[31]

There were, too, in the second quarter of the thirteenth century, the followers of St. Francis and St. Dominic who stirred men's souls with an eloquence which still appealed with its freshness and promise. Like the preachers in colonial New England, the friars were "up and down the land . . . with utopias in their brains and the voice of God in their ears,"[32] urging men to new forms of Christian duty, to obedience and responsibility.

The Church was, moreover, a very integral part of society. The great prelates held lands of the king; they had seignorial responsibilities and were an inseparable part of the feudal structure. Regularly present at the meetings of the king's council, they took part with the barons in consultations and helped reach decisions. Moreover, the clergy was involved in the taxes which were levied; and as the most solvent class in medieval society, they were frequently called upon for what were politely called "gracious" aids.

Laymen and ecclesiastics were constantly involved in the same problems and actions, and the practice of episcopal and baronial coöperation was no brief experiment limited to a regency or a minority. Coöperation was constant in the early thirteenth century, and there is little question but that the model of the complete Christian society of the Church, with its emphasis on general councils, deliberation, and common

[31] J. T. Shotwell, *An Introduction to the History of History* (New York, 1922), p. 324.
[32] P. G. E. Miller, "The Half-Way Covenant," *New England Quarterly* (1933), vi. 676.

ideals, strongly influenced the growth of an organic conception of lay society.

In other ways, equally important, the Church affected the outlook of lay society towards its institutions. Because men live largely by their faiths and dreams, those ideals need constant reinforcement in the face of the inconsistencies presented by change. The craving for permanence and stability in a world that is forever changing results in the creation of fictions and myths to explain what is in terms of what has been, and to rationalize the discrepancies. The process is unconscious up to a point, but it is no less clear that dogma and faiths about institutions are essential if the institutions are to survive. Today it is the economists, the political scientists, and the editorial writers who are the high priests of our institutions; they elaborate our folklore with fictions and verbal explanations. In the Middle Ages this task belonged to the Church, with its monopoly of brains and learning.

So the sentiments men held about such things as law and the king were enforced and elaborated by reference to the Christian revelation. Although the rights enjoyed by the king were little more than intensified private rights, those rights were to some extent idealized by the Church by elaborating the dignities surrounding the office. The king was said to rule by the grace of God, *non sub homine sed sub Deo et lege*. He was anointed at his coronation by the Church, and he took over the kingship as a sacred trust. The power of the English king was thus enhanced and perpetuated by explanations which were at once simple and familiar, yet above all sacred, to the sentiments of ordinary people. The process of dignifying and dramatizing the superior position goes on all the time everywhere, largely unconsciously. It is an important method, says a noted business executive, "of dignifying *all* connection with the organization."[33] In a political organization nothing could be more important. The authority of the royal govern-

[33] C. I. Barnard, *The Functions of the Executive* (Cambridge, Mass., 1938), p. 181.

ment won its acceptance as any government must—that is, through reliance on the normal sentiments of normal people.

Much of the political writing of the thirteenth century in England was an attempt to justify the transformations which were taking place in lay society. Thus we find the statement, "If the king shall be without a bridle, that is, without law, the magnates ought to put a bridle upon him."[34] The author of the Song of Lewes writes, "The king must rule with the aid of his magnates, remembering that he is God's servant. . . . The Divine law supplies the light by which the king must walk."[35] One of the best examples, perhaps, comes from the great Bishop of Lincoln, Robert Grosseteste. Princes and secular judges, he says, cannot establish laws contrary to the law of God, or enjoy laws so established, except by rebelling against God the Father and the Church, to their perpetual damnation and the subversion of the state.[36]

Throughout the thirteenth century, deliberation between the king and his barons becomes increasingly usual. Consultations take on an air that is not merely legal but political. The principle of frequent consultation is one which is asserted and reasserted, justified and explained, not only in political writings but in actual practice. In the so-called Laws of Edward the Confessor, dating from the end of the twelfth century, it is stated that the king should in all matters act with the advice of his barons.[37] The notion that there was an obligation on the part of the barons to share in the government became increasingly marked as the century progressed,[38] and the long minority of Henry III did much to

34 Bracton, De Legibus (ed. Woodbine), ii. 110. This, again, is part of the disputed passage referred to above, note 16. Nevertheless it represents the political views of certain sections of mid-thirteenth-century English society.
35 The Song of Lewes (ed. Kingsford: Oxford, 1890), p. 139. Cf. Introduction, pp. xxvi-xxviii.
36 Roberti Grosseteste Episcopi Lincolniensis Epistolae (ed. Luard, Rolls Series: London, 1861), p. 94.
37 Leges Edwardi Confessoris, xi. 1: "Debet etiam rex omnia rite facere in regno et per judicium procerum regni." Liebermann, Gesetze, i. 635.
38 For illustrations indicating the extent to which the barons were consulted, see H. G. Richardson, Transactions of the Royal Historical Society, 4th ser. (1946), xxviii. 24, note 1.

advance the practical importance of their functions. The barons, in turn, came to regard that obligation as a duty they were bound to fulfill. In the 1250's the barons write to Pope Alexander IV to explain that Henry III has submitted himself to the counsel of the magnates, without whom he is unable to govern his kingdom. It is further stated that the republic is a body, whose members must be knit together; it grows to the benefit of God's working, is moved by the decision of the highest equity, and is ruled by the moderating guidance of reason, by the community of the realm of England.[39] The word "community" had become as much of a rally-call in the thirteenth century as "organized labor" has today. When the magnates are not consulted, they express surprise. They complained because they were not consulted about the imperial marriage of 1236 and the Poitevin alliance in 1242. This feeling of the importance of counsel and consent, that the king and his barons are one, is a dominant feature of the social pattern of the thirteenth century. It gave impetus to the development of parliamentary institutions.

The clear and immediate result of the increased emphasis which came to be placed on counsel and consent was the increase in importance of the king's council. Anyone who glances at the massive indices of the Curia Regis Rolls can see at once the quantity of business which came before the council in the reigns of John and Henry III. As the complexities of the administration grew, with the extension of royal power, more and more matters were taken up by the council, or reserved for them. But hand in hand with the increase in agenda went, naturally enough, a demand for more frequent meetings. It was clear that men were needed who were in a sense civil servants, who could address most of their energies to the task of a quasi-permanent session. The occasional plenary meetings of the council, to which most of the great magnates would be called, were too unwieldy and

39 *Matthaei Parisiensis Chronica Majora*, vi. 400-405.

assembled too infrequently. Consequently we find in the 1220's and 1230's what seems to be a small permanent council of officials, whose standing has been won by efficient service. Skilled in the writs and rolls of the Chancery and the Exchequer, they are "engaged by every interest to forward the crown's official policy."[40] As early as 1237, there are clearly two councils—the large *magnum consilium* and the small *curia regis:* the former meets only when it is summoned by the king, whereas the latter is in almost constant session.

The magnates, pushed progressively into the position of spectators, resented this exclusion. A century and a half of enforced attendance at the king's councils, and the long political education acquired there, had given them a stake in the administration which they were reluctant to let go.[41] But because common consent had become something the king might have reason to dislike, something that was not always the favorable advice he wished to hear, Henry III took the view that he was justified in having a council which would further unremittingly the interests of the crown. Thus the division between the large and the smaller council was indicative of a much more real cleavage between the king and the baronage. The old equilibrium was clearly breaking down. Already critics of the administration because of their inclusion within it, the barons had lost their old standing and not yet acquired a new one. The habits of feudal counsel were ingrained and would need to be broken before an opposition could crystallize. But when the traditional union of king and his magnates was ended, when the feudal equilibrium was destroyed, the way was open for a fight for supremacy between two rival theories of kingship.

The breach was accentuated by Henry's wastefulness, his increasing demands for money, and his wild schemes for foreign domination. Foreigners flocked about the court, and royal favorites received the honors and the offices. Resent-

ment ran particularly high against the tyranny of corrupt
officials, "who pressed to the uttermost point every advantage
given to them by the letter of an obsolete law or the intricate
details of some forgotten custom."[42] Discontent was evident
among the lesser landowners and in the towns, on whom the
burdens of taxation and corruption chiefly fell. In 1257 came
a severe famine; corn was unobtainable or prohibitively high,
and hundreds died in the fields and along the roadsides. A
few months later the crisis came. The baronage rose against
the king, and Henry was forced to give way.

The crisis of 1258 is important from several angles. The
plan of reform sponsored by the barons was no paper constitution; it contained perfectly definite proposals for an efficient, honest administration. It established as a matter of
actual practice that the monarchy was not absolute but was a
monarchy limited by the traditional practices of counsel and
consent. A very hard bargain was driven with Henry: a committee of twenty-four drew up the ordinances of reform which
were submitted and ratified by a full parliament of the magnates. By those ordinances, the kingship was virtually put
into commission: that is, the king continued to reign, but
the barons became self-appointed advisers and ruled in his
name. There was no attempt to abolish the kingship or to
depose the king, no attempt to undo the work of the king's
courts or the king's chancery. There was no idea of setting
up a rival administration. The objective political authority,
in other words, was not destroyed. Everything was done with
the utmost show of legality. The plan was, to use a loose
phrase, a constitutional program of reform.

One of the significant things about the crisis is that the
barons were able to act as a more or less unified body, representing, in their eyes, the community of the realm of England. In 1215, after the Great Charter had been won, the
baronage had not been able to carry on in the minority of
Henry III. Their training in political responsibility had not

42 Treharne, *The Baronial Plan of Reform*, pp. 41-42.

gone far enough, and it is figures like Stephen Langton and St. Edmund—the great ecclesiastics of the day—who maintained the administration in the difficult days which followed the death of King John. In 1258 the baronage was far from inchoate at the time of the crisis, whereas the Church was wholly absorbed in the defense of its own privileges and in asserting the claims of a rigid ecclesiastical caste. The great figures are laymen like Hugh Bigod, Henry of Wingham, Philip Lovel, and above all Simon de Montfort, who considered himself heir to the political ideas of Robert Grosseteste. The lay community, in other words, had become politically self-conscious. It was a fundamental step in the direction of self-government.

The plan of reform was nevertheless a failure, if by failure it is meant that the baronial commission failed to retain power. The unity of the magnates was real only up to a point, for they lacked wide support among all classes of people. It was impossible to marshal local forces successfully against the king, and party feeling ran high everywhere. Louis IX, the greatest idealist of his time, denounced the revolt as immoral and as a severe detraction from the dignity of the crown.[43] Within five years Henry was able to proclaim himself free. The *Dictum de Kenilworth,* promulgated at the end of the baronial revolt in 1266, declares that Henry "shall fully possess, obtain, and fully exercise his Dominion, Authority, and Power Royal: without the let or gainsaying of any, whereby the Royal Dignity may be hurt, contrary to the approved Rights and Laws, and Customs of the Realm long established."[44] The declaration struck a note which was to be dominant in the next reign.

In other respects, however, the reform movement was not a failure. Under the baronial council, the administration, especially on the side of local government, had been coordinated to a degree unknown since the early days of John. The entire existing organization had been completely over-

[43] Stubbs, *Select Charters,* p. 395.
[44] *Statutes of the Realm,* i. 12.

hauled. Much of that organization was retained by the king thereafter. The baronial council had sent justices about from county to county with commissions to enquire into the abuses of officials. They had not been sent, as in the past, for the purpose of extending the royal power and of increasing the revenues of the crown, but with the idea of curbing mal-administration and corruption. Juries of knights had been empaneled in every vill to draw up lists of crimes and abuses for preceding years. Petitions had been solicited from aggrieved persons, and men had been invited to bring appeals before the council. It had also been established that there should be three regular meetings of the general council, for which the word "parliament" is used.

Much of the machinery so devised was retained even after the baronial committee had been completely stripped of its power. Reliance was placed increasingly on committees of local knights for coördinating the central with the local ad-ministration—a step which brought the knights more into prominence and provided them with experience which would in time prove indispensable to them as they came to be sum-moned to parliament. Parliament, which had taken definite form in 1258, was not eclipsed, and "henceforward we have to do with an institution of a distinctive kind . . . which will have a legible and continuous history."[45] Petitions continued to be presented to the council, to be dealt with in time of parliament, so that in the beginning parliament became asso-ciated with the redress of private grievances.

The plan of reform had accepted the distinction between a permanent advisory council close to the king, in which authority was concentrated, and the general council of mag-nates, which met only occasionally. Upon Henry's resump-tion of power that division was maintained, with the result that the power and influence of the general council of mag-nates was considerably diminished. The king administered the complexities of his government through his small council,

45 H. G. Richardson, *Transactions of the Royal Historical Society*, 4th ser. (1946), xxviii. 23.

which was, in effect, a small and efficient civil service made up of judges and other close advisers. But the independence which the magnates, as a group, had achieved during the preceding years was not altogether lost. The king continued to summon them to the parliaments which he called periodically to afforce his small, permanent council. Although the purpose of those parliaments was primarily judicial, the magnates gave their counsel which voiced the opinion of the community of England. That voice was not often loud, but it was audible. Although the feudal notion that counsel involved agreements and coöperation between the king and his tenants-in-chief had disappeared, the idea had not lost hold that many important matters affecting the realm required the approval of the general council meeting in parliament. In 1280 Edward I answered a clerical petition in parliament, saying that he could not do otherwise without departing from the advice of his magnates—a thing which would be profitable neither to himself, nor the Church, nor the realm of England.[46] If counsel had come to mean something which was critical and independent, it had also become something which the king could not do wholly without.

As an institution, then, parliament existed in the reign of Henry III, in form little different from what it was to be after representatives came to be added in the reign of Edward I. The complete absence of sudden innovation in the history of the institution must also be plain. Its origins go back to the dim past of the witanagemot in Saxon days; its growth was nurtured by practices which were completely feudal, and was given direction by the influence of the Christian society of the Church. Its later development in the middle thirteenth century was furthered, not by sentiments of democracy, but by antagonisms bred of the growing incompetence of the king.

46 See E. B. Graves, *English Historical Review* (1928), xliii. 13, note 3.

3

COMPULSORY SELF-GOVERNMENT

THE political equilibrium which had prevailed in the feudal society of England in the early thirteenth century broke down towards the middle of Henry III's reign. The constant and reasoned coöperation which had characterized the relations between the king and the magnates failed; it failed chiefly because of Henry's inefficiency and his reluctance to allow his barons to continue further to share the responsibilities of government. Feudalism, as a basis for the organization of government, was collapsing.

But if feudal principles were losing hold, other formulae were being devised to take their place. The thirteenth century was a time of prosperity, "the culmination of a movement of economic expansion several centuries old."[1] Production was increasing and prices were rising. The landed gentry were growing rich, and it was becoming plain that there were "highly important persons among the subtenants, whereas not all the tenants-in-chief were among the 'great men' of the kingdom."[2] The growth of trade had further marked out the townsfolk as an important, if heretofore neglected, class. If the magnates were participating progressively less in the work of government, there were new groups which had come into prominence and to which the king might turn.

From the standpoint of the history of parliament, one of the significant developments of the thirteenth century is the king's recognition of the importance of the undertenants and the men of the towns, and his summoning them to treat with him in parliament. The appearance in parliament of knights

[1] G. C. Homans, *English Villagers of the Thirteenth Century* (Cambridge, Mass., 1942), p. 36.
[2] D. Pasquet, *Essai sur les origines de la Chambre des Communes* (Paris, 1914), p. 15.

and burgesses, who represented the counties and boroughs, marks the feeble beginnings of the house of commons. It is therefore pertinent to ask for what purposes the king recognized their importance and in what way they became associated with the work of government. Liberal historians of the Victorian era have pointed to the summoning of knights and burgesses to parliament as a step consciously taken by the king towards the establishment of constitutional government.[3] On principle, however, we must guard against the assumption that the growth of a middle class necessarily means the growth of democratic feeling—an assumption which may be superficially accurate, but which obscures organic processes. We must, too, guard against the assumption that in England self-government came about because people wished to rule themselves and strove successfully to that end. The inclusion in parliament of representatives of the counties and towns passed entirely unnoticed by contemporary chroniclers. That fact of itself suggests that the development was in line with perfectly well-known practices which antedate the general summons to parliament.

From Saxon times, local government in England had centered in the ancient divisions of the shire and hundred, in the county court and in the hundred court. Those local institutions were not only strengthened but perpetuated by the early Norman rulers, whose government immediately after the Conquest was in the nature of a military occupation. They had not time to work out new machinery, and they seized upon existing forms. Needless to say, the new rule was made more palatable to the English by the perpetuation of institutions to which they had been long accustomed. William the Conqueror and Henry I both issued ordinances to the effect that the courts of the shire and the hundred should meet as they had in the time of Edward the Confessor, "and not otherwise."[4]

3 For example, Stubbs, *Constitutional History*, ii. 305.
4 Liebermann, *Gesetze*, i. 488, 524.

Every freeholder in England was a freeholder both of his county and of his hundred. Just as a great tenant-in-chief was bound to attend the king's court as a suitor, so every freeholder of the county was obliged to attend his county court; every three weeks he was bound to appear at his hundred court. The duties of the suitors in those courts were various, but chief among them was their function as doomsmen. It was their task to "find" the law, to ascertain a custom, for law at that time was conceived of as the custom of those who enjoyed it. Just as in the king's court, or in the court of an honour, judgment was pronounced by the suitors, by the barons in attendance, so in the local courts a judgment was rendered by the suitors who had knowledge of local custom. There was no judge in our sense, who gave the opinion of the court. It was a widespread medieval notion that law was something already in existence, to be found but not made.[5] In Viollet's words, law was something you would ask of your neighbor, as you would borrow fire or water.

Other obligations fell upon the freeholders of the county, apart from suit at court. They were required to join in the hue and cry, or the *posse comitatus*, in pursuit of the murderer or the thief. They were expected to report to the coroner a murder, or the finding of a corpse. Such communal duties were by no means inconsiderable, and in no way could they be avoided. The performance of those duties ensured the stability and continuity of the local government of medieval England. In effect, it was compulsory self-government.

The possibility of developing and utilizing the ancient practices for purposes of coördinating local institutions with the expanding machinery of the royal government greatly impressed itself upon the early Norman kings. If such practices could be coördinated with the work of the royal administration, it would greatly enhance the king's prestige at the expense of baronial power. One of the methods by which that

[5] See F. Kern, "Recht und Verfassung im Mittelalter," *Historische Zeitschrift* (1919), cxx. 1.

coördination was achieved was by the use of the jury. A distinctly Continental importation, the jury soon became a regular means of communication between the king's officials and the local communities. From the time of the Domesday survey, fiscal inquests, requiring local knowledge, were conducted on a large scale.[6] After the introduction of justices in eyre by Henry II, local juries were employed on an ever-widening scale. The general eyre became one of the principal links in the "mighty chain forged by the Angevin kings whereby the frame of government was held together and the local institutions of England were made to contribute their share to the centralized polity of the Normans."[7] Juries were empaneled in the county court for the presentment of criminals and to report on other matters affecting the interests of the crown.[8] Moreover, inquests conducted by men of the county were required to be held after the death of any of the king's tenants-in-chief, for the purpose of valuing rents and other income due from the land. Local men might also be put under oath to give a verdict on the extent of damage, loss, or waste incurred during the holding of a wardship. Or again, the king might wish an estimate on the costs of travel, of garrisoning a town, or of taking waste land under cultivation. For all those purposes a jury might be empaneled.

The men of the towns were no less involved in the performance of similar local duties on behalf of the king. In the course of time, exemptions were purchased of the crown, but not before the required duties and services had accumulated precedents of obedience and habits which were nurtured by growing community life.

It is easy to see how these varied services, long-continued and unpaid, wrought special aptitudes and developed ways of reacting to recurring conditions and problems. The services which were exacted constantly demanded estimate, discrimi-

6 C. H. Haskins, *Norman Institutions* (Cambridge, Mass., 1918), p. 234.
7 H. M. Cam, *Studies in the Hundred Rolls* (Oxford, 1921), p. 9.
8 Cf. the agenda of the justices' eyre in 1194. Stubbs, *Select Charters*, pp. 252 ff.

nation, and judgment. Their performance was a kind of political education; it was a rigorous training in self-government at the king's command.[9] The curious thing is that the various communal services and local duties were encouraged by autocratic kings who had no idea of educating the freeholders and undertenants to the point where they could one day take an effective part in the direction of government. The Norman and Plantagenet kings aimed simply and solely at carrying on the government with a minimum of officials and at consolidating further their own power.

As the twelfth century came to a close, the duties which the crown exacted from the freeholders fell increasingly on the class of tenants known as the knights of the shire. Those knights were county landowners who had considerable local prestige and were frequently persons of considerable means. As early as the reign of Richard I we find them taking the place of barons on the special commissions which supplemented the eyres.[10] In the thirteenth century we find them assigned to commissions for the tallaging of the king's demesne, for breaches of the peace, or for enforcing the Assize of Arms. They also served on the grand juries of presentment which "presented" to the itinerant justices the crimes committed in the county since the last eyre. If a case which involved a particularly serious crime or the special interest of the crown arose when the justices were not within the county, measures had to be taken to bring the case before them. On the one hand, that might involve searching out the justices while on circuit in some other county; on the other hand, it might mean taking the case to Westminster, where the judges customarily sat. In both instances the "record" of the court where the proceedings had started was carried before the justices by knights selected for the purpose from among the suitors.

9 This thesis has been vividly presented by A. B. White, *Self-Government at the King's Command* (St. Paul, 1933).
10 Jolliffe, *Constitutional History*, p. 313.

Many of those practices appear to be in use as early as the reign of Henry II. The Assize of Clarendon, in 1166, prescribes that when the sheriff brings violators of the assize before the itinerant justices, he shall bring along with them "two legal men to bear the record from the county and the hundred where they were arrested."[11] Examples increase in the late twelfth and early thirteenth century. In 1194, the king's court orders the sheriff of Wiltshire to have an inquest made with regard to land, the tenure of which is contested; and he is told to send the result to Westminster by four knights.[12] When a judgment of the county has to be defended before the king's justices against the appeal of a dissatisfied litigant, "four knights come in the name of the county, to bear the 'record' and to 'defend' the judgment."[13] In short, when the king's court needs information to proceed on a case; when the facts about succession or possession need recognizing; when the record of an inquest must be shown—in all such matters, the county sends the record of the facts by four knights. As Professor Adams says, the practices of the early thirteenth century show "a direct line of connection between the county court and the king's council, already established and in frequent use."[14]

Although the task of bearing the county record fell upon the knights of the shire, as did many of the duties involving the relations between the central and the local government, the towns were frequently called upon to send legal men before the justices or up to Westminster. Boroughs might be asked to present the accounts of their farm to the Exchequer,[15] or they might be required to show a charter or prove a privilege in justification of an alleged violation.[16] In 1231

---

[11] Assize of Clarendon, c. 4. Stubbs, *Select Charters*, p. 170.

[12] *Rotuli Curiae Regis* (ed. Palgrave: London, 1835), i. 44.

[13] Pasquet, *Essai sur les origines de la Chambre des Communes*, p. 31.

[14] G. B. Adams, *The Origin of the English Constitution* (New Haven, 1912), pp. 321-322.

[15] *Dialogus de Scaccario* (ed. Hughes, Crump and Johnson: Oxford, 1902), p. 80.

[16] *Rotuli Chartarum* (ed. Hardy: London, 1837), 57, 65.

the sheriff of Yorkshire is directed to summon before the justices, when they come next into the county, not only the higher clergy, the barons, the knights and freeholders of the county, but also twelve legal burgesses from each borough, and all others who "usually come and who ought to come."[17]

The expense and annoyance to the county and the town, as well as to the individual, is obvious. The king's insistence on the performance of such services was therefore regarded as an abuse. However, the king had the right to inflict a penalty on the county if the record were not produced on the appointed day, or if the group of knights were not complete. Similarly, a borough might be fined if its legal representatives were not present. That right of compelling the burgesses and the knights to appear at Westminster when called upon the king did not hesitate to exercise.

Apart from the training in self-government which it provided, the work of the knights of the shire and of the burgesses may, at first sight, appear to have little to do with their later summons to parliament. In the duties they performed, however, and in the manner they performed them, are implicit precedents of very considerable importance for the future. In the first place, the counties were not always called up to Westminster individually, nor were they always summoned solely for judicial purposes. In 1213, King John summoned four knights from each county "to discuss the affairs of the kingdom."[18] In 1226, the sheriffs of eight counties received orders to provide for the election in each county of four of the more discreet knights, who were to meet to discuss the disputed interpretation of some articles of Magna Carta.[19] Again, in the following year, similar instructions were sent to the sheriffs of thirty-five counties.[20] As precedents for the later summons to parliament to act on behalf of the counties, those early assemblies were of no small significance.

17 Stubbs, *Select Charters,* p. 354.
18 *Ibid.,* p. 282.
19 *Ibid.,* p. 353.
20 *Rotuli Litterarum Clausarum* (ed. Hardy: London, 1844), ii. 212-13.

The first summoning of knights to parliament in 1254 was a repetition of the earlier procedure for the express purpose of granting an aid.

It should also be noted that from the time of Henry II onwards there was a growing disposition on the part of the king to deal with the counties and towns as communities rather than as aggregates of individuals. That tendency was fostered by prevailing medieval notions about the importance of groups, but it was given impetus by the introduction of the system of justices itinerant. From a composite of competing and often independent jurisdictions, the county was suddenly given unity and began to grow in a new way at the expense of feudal franchises. Every man in the county, of whatever fee, was thereafter at the disposal of the justices' inquest, and the royal bailiffs were given entry to every city, borough, and honour.[21] Its unity was such that by the second decade of the thirteenth century "the shire was summoned to the justiciars' sessions to hear and obey the king's commands at large—*ad audiendum et faciendum,* as in the later writs of parliament."[22] The sense of unity and independence of the feudal scheme was even stronger in the boroughs, where privileges of self-government and other immunities had been bought from the crown. By the thirteenth century the important boroughs were largely independent of the jurisdiction of the counties within which they were situated, so that "a new line had to be drawn between the boroughs and other *communitates.*"[23] The king recognized the communal unity of the counties and the towns not only for the administrative purposes which have been outlined but also for his own political purposes. We have had occasion to observe the importance of the role which the idea of "community" played in the development of the baronial opposi-

---

21 Assize of Clarendon, c. 11. Stubbs, *Select Charters,* p. 171
22 Jolliffe, *Constitutional History,* p. 307.
23 F. Pollock and F. W. Maitland, *History of English Law* (Cambridge, 1911), i. 687.

tion in Henry III's reign.[24] The principles implicit in that idea were further exploited by the king, whose recognition of the communities of the shires helped him to rebut the claim of the barons that they alone represented the community of England.[25] The attribution of the characteristics of a community to those groups "gave a new non-feudal colour to the administrative organization of the provinces, and it had an influence upon the growth of parliamentary estates which is difficult to analyse but none the less real."[26] By the time of Edward II the representatives of the counties and towns in parliament are themselves referred to as the *communitas regni.*[27]

Of fundamental importance in the services which the knights of the shire, and to a lesser extent the burgesses, rendered to the king was the development of the principle of representation. From as early as the eleventh and twelfth centuries we can recognize that principle in operation in the local courts, where a few persons acquit whole communities of their burden of suit.[28] Each township, for example, was customarily represented in the hundred court and in the county court by six men at the outside. Similarly, although only a small proportion of the county was present at a meeting of the county court, the county court was the county. Action taken by the county court was equivalent to action taken by the whole county. It is relevant, moreover, to note that the same Latin word, *comitatus,* means both "county" and "county court." As Professor McIlwain says, "the fiction of 'representation' alone can explain this identity. There

24 Above, Chapter II.
25 Cf. Jolliffe, *Constitutional History,* pp. 329-31.
26 *Ibid.,* p. 329.
27 Cf. *ibid.,* pp. 330-31.
28 Cf. Leges Henrici Primi, VII. 7: "Si quis baronum regis vel aliorum comitatui secundum legem interfuerit, totam terram quam illic in dominio suo habet, acquietare poterit. Eodem modo est si dapifer ejus legitime fuerit. Si uterque necessario desit, praepositus et sacerdos et quatuor de melioribus villae assint pro omnibus qui nominatim non erunt ad placitum submoniti." Stubbs, *Select Charters,* p. 124.

must have been in existence some theory of representation as well as the fact."[29]

When a case was drawn by royal writ out of a manorial or communal court into the king's court, the latter required the record to be brought up from the court where the proceedings had begun. The record was generally rot written but "was only in the minds of the men of the court;"[30] hence, bringing up the record to the king's court meant a bringing of men. The knights who went before the itinerant justices, or to Westminster, and spoke for the county court were considered to be speaking in the name of the county. That is why the county was bound by their action, and why through them the county could be treated as a unit; why, even, it could be required to appear as a suitor at the king's court. Because representation was a practice entirely characteristic of local justice and local government long before the first summoning of parliament, there was really nothing new when the king made use of such practices on a larger scale and summoned county representatives to treat with him on the affairs of the kingdom. Just as four men and the reeve had represented the township in the county court, so in 1213 four men and the sheriff could represent the county in a national assembly summoned by the king.[31]

A recent writer on representative government has declared that "the church originated representative institutions; the state adopted them."[32] The thesis has obtained some currency through the writings of Professor Ernest Barker,[33] who considers that the use of representation in the English national

29 *Cambridge Medieval History* (Cambridge, 1932), vii. 668.

30 *Ibid.*, p. 669. That the record was occasionally in writing is shown by documents emanating from the county court. See C. H. Jenkinson, *Cambridge Historical Journal* (1923), i. 105.

31 Stubbs, *Select Charters*, p. 282: "quatuor discretos milites de comitatu tuo illuc venire facias ad nos . . . ad loquendum nobiscum de negotiis regni nostri." The word "homines," instead of "milites," appears in Stubbs' quotation by mistake. The original record reads "milites." See A. E. Levett, *English Historical Review* (1916), xxxi. 85.

32 H. J. Ford, *Representative Government* (New York, 1924), p. 111.

33 E. Barker, *The Dominican Order and Convocation* (Oxford, 1913).

assemblies was adopted from the methods used for the representation of the cathedral chapters and the parochial clergy in church synods. According to Barker, the practice of representation in ecclesiastical assemblies derives from the procedure of the Dominicans in assembling the general chapters of their order. The difficulty with Barker's thesis lies in the fact that there were no Dominicans in England before 1221; and yet, in 1213, eight years earlier, there are recorded the writs by which King John summoned four knights from each county "to discuss the affairs of the kingdom."[34] Those summonses were issued thirteen years before the first proctors of the cathedral chapters were summoned to an ecclesiastical assembly.

In view of the fundamental weakness of Barker's thesis, we must discard the idea that representation came from the Church and that ecclesiastical assemblies were the model for parliamentary assemblies. On the other hand, we must not overlook the possibility of some ecclesiastical influence in giving currency to the representative principle. The practice of lay and ecclesiastical coöperation in the first half of the thirtenth century, discussed in the preceding chapter, is of first importance. And we can at least conjecture that in that great age of enthusiasms the influence of the Church's habits of organized action must have left its impress on the lay mind. The clergy, too, had long understood the principle which was later to become the foundation of parliamentary enactment, that the validity of decisions depended on the willing acceptance of those concerned, or of their representatives.

The Church clearly gave currency, even in the lay world, to many ideas of Roman and Canon law; both those systems have a good deal to say of procuratorial powers and the law of agency. Moreover, as Dr. Otto Hintze has pointed out with considerable acuteness, although representative assemblies have generally evolved out of conditions of feudalism, they are nevertheless characteristic only of those countries which

---

[34] Stubbs, *Select Charters*, p. 282.

were at one time Roman Catholic.[35] Feudalism has obtained in some form in Egypt, in the Moslem world, and in Japan. Yet in none of those countries did feudalism give rise to representative assemblies.

Accordingly the possible influence of the Church in promoting the extension of representative institutions in the thirteenth century cannot be overlooked. But to suggest an influence is not to account for the first cause. Two main questions must be answered. How did the practices which have been outlined come to be extended on a national scale? How, in the second place, did they become associated with parliament and, from an occasional expedient, become a permanent feature of that institution?

The real motives which prompted the king regularly to summon representatives of the counties and towns to treat with himself and his council on the affairs of the kingdom have been the subject of considerable discussion in the last fifty years. The old, and now discredited, view of Bishop Stubbs pretended that a wise and provident king—Edward I —foresaw the advantages to be gained by democratic government, and took his subjects into coöperation with him.[36] It was alleged, therefore, that the house of commons was created in 1295 in order to loose the chains which had bound in the primitive and Anglo-Saxon urge to self-government. Another view, supported by plausible if untenable arguments, suggests that administrative expedience was the important factor. Dr. Ludwig Riess argued persuasively that by summoning representatives to parliament on a regular basis the king would be able better to supervise local government by means of representatives, who were to bring petitions of grievances to parliament and take back to their "constituencies" the council's replies and administrative orders.[37] Attractive

35 O. Hintze, "Weltgeschichtliche Bedingungen der Repräsentativverfassung," *Historische Zeitschrift* (1930), cxliii. 1.
36 Stubbs, *Constitutional History*, ii. 305.
37 L. Riess, *Geschichte des Wahlrechts zum englischen Parlament im Mittelalter* (Leipzig, 1885). See also his article in *Historische Zeitschrift*, Neue Folge (1888), xxiv. 1.

as that theory may at first glance appear,[38] it cannot be supported by the evidence, which shows that the knights and burgesses presented very few petitions in the early parliaments, and that those they did present were concerned to a minimum with complaints against royal officials.[39]

Most scholars are now agreed that, although the knights and burgesses could be useful to the king in acting as his agents or in giving occasional advice on matters of importance to local government, the crown's need of money was the most immediate reason for summoning representatives of the counties and towns to parliament.[40]

At the beginning of the thirteenth century, the revenues of the king of England may be described as ordinary and extraordinary. The ordinary revenue consisted of: (1) The county farm, which was a fixed sum paid by the sheriff for the privilege of farming the county revenue; (2) the lump sums paid by certain towns for similar privileges; (3) the proceeds of justice, and the fines imposed by the king's justices; (4) the income from feudal incidents, such as wardships, reliefs, and so forth.

The extraordinary revenues consisted first of all of the three regular feudal aids. Those involved a contribution to be given on the occasion of the knighting of the king's eldest son, the once marrying of his eldest daughter, and the ransoming of the king's person, if he were taken in battle. In addition, there was scutage, a composition levied on those military tenants who preferred to commute their obligations, rather than serve in the army. There were also contributions, called tallages, which the king occasionally levied on his demesne. Finally, there were sums taken less often from Jews and re-

---

[38] It has been accepted in part by Pasquet, *Essai sur les origines de la Chambre des Communes,* pp. 234, 241.

[39] G. L. Haskins, "The Petitions of Representatives in the Parliaments of Edward I," *English Historical Review* (1938), liii. 1.

[40] J. G. Edwards, in *Oxford Essays in Medieval History Presented to H. E. Salter* (Oxford, 1934), p. 147; C. Stephenson, in *Haskins Anniversary Essays* (Boston, 1929), pp. 311-12, note 45.

ligious houses and which were politely known as "gifts" or "aids."

By the thirteenth century, those sources of income had become, through force of custom and precedent, fairly fixed and stereotyped. They were incapable of yielding much more. At the same time they were found to be insufficient for royal needs. In the first place, the revenues were always in arrears and were never completely paid up.[41] Moreover, the great development of the machinery of government under Henry II, the numerous wars, the crusade of Richard in the Holy Land, to say nothing of the wastefulness of John's and Henry III's administration—all those factors had resulted in outlays which far exceeded the receipts. Finally, the sharp rise in prices of the thirteenth century had enormously increased the crown's difficulties.

The incidence of taxation supposedly fell only upon the tenants-in-chief, but in practice it had come to fall also on the undertenants. Proportionately, the taxes were so large that the great landowners could assume that their own tenants would help them, as in fact they did, and in turn spread out the assessment on their own holdings. These taxes, although levied with the consent of the tenants-in-chief alone, were paid ultimately by the undertenants as well, and hence they "helped to form the idea of a general tax, taken for the needs of the government and paid by all who were in its care."[42] They perhaps contributed something to the growing political self-consciousness of the lesser landowners. In time, at least, the undertenants insisted that they had a right to a voice in the levy of the tax. For that reason, the regular forms of extraordinary taxation are important, even if the real development was to begin elsewhere.

The beginnings of what we may call modern taxation were in the gracious aid which a lord was privileged to ask of his

41 See S. K. Mitchell, *Studies in Taxation Under John and Henry III* (New Haven, 1914), pp. 2-3.
42 *Ibid.*, p. 351.

vassals to relieve his wants under extraordinary circumstances. Gracious aids were never levied by the crown on a national scale before the reign of Richard I, but they had been used constantly by the barons on their own holdings. Beginning as an emergency expedient in the reigns of Richard I and John, aids were demanded with increasing frequency in the reign of Henry III.[43] Apart from their later history, three things are striking about gracious aids. In the first place, they had the advantage of elasticity; in the second place, because they were "gracious," they required the consent of those who were to pay them. Finally, they were assessed not on land but on personal property. In a period of great economic expansion, such as characterized the thirteenth century, this last fact was one of importance. It meant that all sources of wealth, especially in the new moneyed classes, could be tapped, and that the revenue would increase proportionately with the wealth of the community.

The growing feeling of the importance of consent in the thirteenth century, together with the specific idea that gracious aids required the assent of those who paid them, gave a marked impetus to parliamentary institutions. The substitution of a tax which was national, for one which was feudal, helped to break down the monopoly of consent enjoyed by the magnates. In the early thirteenth century, the gracious aids were consented to only by the magnates and tenants-in-chief. The principle had been established by the demand of the barons in 1215, that all such extraordinary aids, as well as scutages, should be imposed only by the common counsel of the realm.[44] At that time, the barons constituted the common counsel of the realm, and they were assumed in a vague sense to be acting for the tenants below them. In 1237, for example, it is recited that a *colloquium* had met at Westminster, composed of "the archbishops, bishops, abbots, priors, earls, and barons of our whole realm," and no others. The record then

[43] See W. E. Lunt, *The Valuation of Norwich* (Oxford, 1926), pp. 6-8.
[44] Magna Carta, c. 12.

goes on to say that these same persons, together with "the knights, and freemen, for themselves and their villeins," had granted the king an aid of a thirtieth of their movables.[45]

But as feudal principles began to lose hold, the magnates found it increasingly difficult to collect from their sub-vassals, on to whom they were constantly shifting the actual burden of the exactions. The increasing importance, wealth and strength of the country gentry gave the barons cause to doubt their ability to consent to an aid of which the principal burden would fall upon the undertenants. The crown, pursuing its policy of weakening the power of the magnates, took advantage of those developments and, for purposes of assessment and collection, removed one group of taxpayers after another from the control of the tenants-in-chief. Commissions composed of knights and freeholders in each county became responsible, under the supervision of the sheriff, for collecting the aids and for forwarding the proceeds to the Exchequer.[46] Such methods not only helped further to advance the unity of the county, but they also helped to make the counties into fiscal constituencies. In that manner, there was "created that division between baronial and county assessment which later extended to the right or duty of the two groups, nobility and communes of the counties, each to tax its own order."[47]

By and large, the towns were exempt from the gracious aids, and there was, in the mid-thirteenth century, little pressure to summon them through representatives to consent to such aids. A great many of the cities and boroughs were legally a part of the king's demesne, and they could therefore be tallaged by the king at will. However, because the towns were growing in importance, as their wealth increased, the king's arbitrary right of taxation was limited in practice.

---

45 Stubbs, *Select Charters*, p. 358.
46 Cf. the writ for the collection of the aid of a thirtieth in 1237, *ibid.*, pp. 358-59.
47 Jolliffe, *Constitutional History*, p. 310.

Assessments when made were frequently reduced on the demand of the towns, and many of the larger boroughs compelled the official assessors to accept a fixed amount as the customary limit of their liability.[48] Even in the towns, therefore, we find the notion developing that a tax should be consented to by those who are to pay it.

There were, therefore, indications that the king might have to call together large numbers of the undertenants in order to obtain their consent to aids. Had Henry merely afforced the great council of magnates with prominent knights and freeholders, the development of parliament might have been very different. What he did, when it seemed desirable to consult the undertenants, was to turn to the counties, as units, rather than to the individual landowners. We have noted the development of the counties' unity for administrative, judicial, and fiscal purposes. We have seen, also, that knights, chosen by the county court, were in the habit of coming before the king to bring information and otherwise to speak on behalf of the counties. It was no great innovation for the king to summon knights to appear before him to declare what aid the county would give. Although no evidence exists, it is possible that knights of the shire may have been consulted on the granting of an aid on the various occasions when they were summoned before the council in the early thirteenth century. But the first time we can be sure that the royal government was concerned about obtaining the consent of the undertenants through county representatives, on a nation-wide scale, was in the year 1254. Men and money were needed at that time for a war pending with the king of Castile. Writs were addressed to all the sheriffs to provide for the election of two lawful and discreet knights of each county, elected *ad hoc* by the county, in the name of one and all. They were directed to come to Westminster "to consider together

[48] London, for example, by 1255, had come to regard £1,000 as the limit of its tallage.

with the knights of the other counties whom we have had summoned for the same day, what aid they will be willing to grant us in our great need."[49]

No aid was granted on this occasion, because the Castilian danger disappeared.[50] But a precedent had been set for calling together an assembly on a national scale. Moreover, the knights had been elected in full county court and were expected to bind their counties by their decision at Westminster. In 1258, four years later, a similar assembly was summoned, again for a financial purpose.[51] But, as in 1254, no aid was granted, for the assembly demanded certain reforms as a condition of the grant being made.[52] Presumably the knights refused to commit themselves, declaring that they had to consult their constituents."[53]

In 1258, the year which marks the beginning of the baronial revolt, two precedents had been set—one for the calling of an assembly of representative knights to consent to the granting of an aid, another for refusing to grant the aid until certain projected reforms had been effected. The years 1258 to 1264 witnessed further advances in the prestige of the knights. Attention has been drawn to the increased reliance upon groups of knights during the period of the baronial reform. Because both the baronial reformers and the king's adherents desired the appearance of wide popular support, it became highly important to sound out the feelings of the lesser landowners. During that period the barons and the king vied with each other in an attempt to secure the support of the knights. In 1261 the Bishop of Worcester and the Earls of Leicester and Gloucester summoned an assembly of knights in Henry's name, to appear before them, "to join them in a discussion on the common affairs of the realm."[54] Henry III tried to pre-

49 Stubbs, *Select Charters*, pp. 365-366.
50 *Matthaei Parisiensis Chronica Majora*, v. 440.
51 *Reports from the Lords Committees Touching the Dignity of a Peer of the Realm* (London, 1829), i. 461; ii. 7.
52 See T. Rymer, *Foedera* (London, 1704), i. 654.
53 Pasquet, *Essai sur les origines de la Chambre des Communes*, p. 45.
54 Stubbs, *Select Charters*, pp. 394-95.

vent the meeting by summoning the same knights to treat with him at Windsor on the same day. In the writs he issued to the sheriffs with the new instructions, Henry implied that the appearance of the knights was highly important for undertakings in "the honor and general interest of the kingdom."[55]

Three years later, in 1264, Henry was taken prisoner at the battle of Lewes, and again it was to the knights that the victorious party turned. Simon de Montfort, its leader, caused representatives of the counties to be summoned in the name of the king to treat with the barons on the conditions of a durable peace.[56] But, as in the case of the assemblies immediately preceding, the purpose for which the knights were called was to strengthen the baronial party. Their function was to approve the measures adopted by the magnates. The constitution which was adopted was distinctly aristocratic, therefore, in spite of the reliance placed on the support of the knights and a large popular element from London. No one then dreamed of making parliament a permanent means of controlling the king's government. The greater part of the English people—the barons included—did not show any wish to take over the government of the realm, which they regarded as essentially the business of the king and his council. But, as M. Pasquet says, "they were very discontented with the king and his favorites."[57] Events, therefore, more than principles, urged Simon de Montfort and his party to place their reliance on the lesser gentry and the townsfolk.

In 1265, Earl Simon compelled Henry III to summon a great parliament.[58] Two of the more lawful and discreet knights of the counties were ordered to appear to give their counsel on matters "concerning the community of our realm."[59] In addition, from four to six burgesses were called from certain towns for the same purpose.[60] What the representatives were

55 *Ibid.*
56 *Ibid.*, pp. 399-400.
57 Pasquet, *Essai sur les origines de la Chambre des Communes,* p. 60.
58 Stubbs, *Select Charters,* p. 403.
59 *Reports on the Dignity of a Peer,* i. 143.
60 *Ibid.*

called upon to do at this parliament we do not know. Presumably Simon wanted a general recognition of the new constitution by as many persons as possible.[61] At any rate, he appreciated the inadequacy of a purely baronial assembly, and saw the need for further backing for his program. Only those towns were summoned whose support was certain. There is no proof whatever that Simon intended to set a precedent for other similar assemblies, or that he saw the "uses and glories" to which representative government would ultimately grow.[62] At a moment when general support of his policies seemed most necessary, he convoked an unusual assembly. His idea was "to consolidate against the attacks of the English nobility the quasi-royal power which he held after Lewes."[63] A contemporary of Simon's, the chronicler Thomas Wykes, bluntly writes that Simon wanted merely "to put down the great men and ruin their power, to break the horns of the proud, so that he might the more freely and easily subdue the people, after having destroyed the strength of the magnates."[64] Earl Simon never posed, as posterity has wished him to, as a noble, high-minded and patriotic Englishman. Cadet of a great house, his prestige was firmly rooted in social distinction and was maintained by his ability. But that he was a demagogue can only with difficulty be denied.

The importance of the assembly of 1265 is not that the burgesses were summoned to parliament for the first time. Their summons to a central assembly had precedents in their appearance as representatives before the sessions of the itinerant justices and before the king's courts at Westminster. The significance of de Montfort's famous parliament lies in the fact that for the first time representatives of the counties and towns were called together simultaneously. As a precedent for the future it marks the feeble beginnings of the house

61 Ch. Bémont, *Simon de Montfort* (Paris, 1884), pp. 230-33.
62 Stubbs, *Constitutional History*, ii. 104.
63 Pasquet, *Essai sur les origines de la Chambre des Communes*, p. 73.
64 *Annales Monastici*, iv. 160.

of commons. Moreover, Simon appears to have thought of the assembly as in a sense a great council. The parliament of 1265 accordingly gave a certain definiteness to the new conception of parliament which was beginning to grow up, a conception of a court which would in due course include the commons of the realm as well as the magnates and members of the king's council. Above all, perhaps, the parliament is significant "as a sign that the vast economic and social changes, which in the end determine the legal and the constitutional, . . . were beginning to affect the forms of government."[65]

Not every parliament after 1265 included representatives of the shires or the towns, or of both. Although parliaments continued to be assembled regularly in the later years of Henry III and in the reign of Edward I, knights and burgesses were summoned to only a few of those assemblies. At times they were called to special *ad hoc* assemblies for the granting of an aid or for some other immediate purpose.[66] Eventually, however, they came to be summoned chiefly in time of parliament, and for that development the early experiments in Henry's reign were of high importance. Moreover, the enforced services, judicial and non-judicial, which the crown exacted from the people in local government had developed in the knights and burgesses habits of mind and of action in the realm of government which made them useful to the king and to their localities. Out of their past history they had acquired "a *savoir-faire* which . . . helps to account for parliament's early vitality—they had capacities that any analogous elements in the French estates general possessed in no such measure. This long discipline surely did much to make modern self-government possible."[67]

At no time in the thirteenth century do we find any theorizing about the "rights" of new classes to share in the govern-

[65] Adams, *Origin of the English Constitution*, p. 330.
[66] For examples, see *Parliamentary Writs*, i. 16, 21, 26.
[67] White, *Self-Government at the King's Command*, p. 129.

ment. Nowhere do we see any competition for election to parliament among the knights and burgesses, who would have preferred to stay at home. Nevertheless we can see, as Henry III's reign draws to a close, that the administration is relying increasingly upon the lesser landowners and, to some extent, upon the men of the towns. That this is an important phenomenon we cannot say until it has become a persistent fact. For the present, it must be observed as a factor in the artifice of government in the thirteenth century.

THE COMMONS OF THE REALM
IN PARLIAMENT

T HE classic account of the beginnings of the house of commons is that of the learned Bishop Stubbs. Stubbs's account, however, has been said to resemble the opening chapters of the book of Genesis in two important respects—"it describes an act of creation and it no longer commands general acceptance."[1] Plausible as his theories of how the wise and provident Edward I took the nation into partnership with him may have seemed to the nineteenth century, those theories have today been pretty generally abandoned. Convenient as are the dates of Simon de Montfort's parliament in 1265, and the Model Parliament in 1295, as signifying the definite beginnings of the house of commons, their importance has been greatly overestimated.

An attempt has been made in the preceding chapters to demonstrate that the origins of parliament are to be sought in the social fabric of the twelfth and thirteenth centuries, in institutions and habits of action which were very largely feudal. The reinforcing of parliament with representatives of the counties and towns was a natural consequence of long familiarity with ideas about counsel and consent, together with the increasing administrative needs of the crown. The development was made possible by the extension of practices long familiar to the knights and burgesses, practices which involved a great deal of self-government at the king's command.

The custom of calling regular meetings of parliament was established in the later days of Henry III. There was nothing extraordinary in the fact that Edward I continued the practice of his father in that respect. What induced Edward to

[1] G. Lapsley, *Cambridge Historical Journal* (1936), v. 122.

include knights in those assemblies was first and foremost his need for money. He found that in this way the collection of aids was facilitated, and that more could be collected than was otherwise possible. Moreover, by dealing with the counties as fiscal units for the assessment and collection of aids, he seriously limited the power of the magnates to make grants on behalf of their undertenants. The imposition of that limitation on feudal practice strengthened the king's power by fostering the growth of the idea that people paid taxes as subjects of the crown rather than as vassals of the intermediate lords. Representatives of the towns were also included because Edward saw that it was to his advantage to relinquish his legal rights of tallage and to substitute therefor voluntary consent.[2] "The co-operation of the moneyed classes arising in the towns was of more practical value than literal insistence on what was fast becoming an old-fashioned prerogative."[3] It should also be borne in mind that parliament brought into focus the entire machinery of government at one time. It was convenient to have on hand all who might be needed for consultation in judicial or fiscal matters. The council might find it desirable to have present the knights who filled administrative posts in the county, so that they might give accounts of their stewardships, or bear out the allegations of a petitioner who was appealing from a judgment of the county court. At the same time, prominent burgesses would be able to give some idea of the possibilities of future taxation or the levying of duties and imposts on wool.

The events of the mid-thirteenth century had proven that there were highly important classes of persons in the realm besides the king's tenants-in-chief. At times of crisis it had appeared that those classes could be relied upon for earnest political support. The knights of the shire, as contrasted with

2 G. L. Haskins, *The Statute of York and the Interest of the Commons* (Cambridge, Mass., 1935), pp. 77-78.
3 M. McKisack, *The Parliamentary Representation of English Boroughs during the Middle Ages* (Oxford, 1932), p. 129.

many of the turbulent and selfish nobility, were on the whole the most stable element in the social structure. That has always been true of the landed aristocracy in England. The burgesses, too, as a consequence of their wealth and increasing commercial prominence, had come to be an element in the community which no one—particularly the crown—could afford long to ignore. Moreover, feudalism, as a basis of the organization of government, was collapsing. With it was going the idea of a society living by an inherited law, a law which was thought of largely as custom, which was not enacted by either the king or magnates, but affirmed by them together in the common council of the realm. "The basic conception of law as custom is shaken, it is a time of confusion as to the ultimate authority from which the new law which is not custom comes."[4] Even among contemporaries extreme and contradictory views prevailed. "The age is committed to a search for something radically new in its policy"—on the one hand, a legislator, if the change was to be radical and was to bear down on the feudal rights of the past; on the other hand, a revival of feudal councils on a much broader basis, if the older view of the popularism of law was to prevail.[5]

Such was the situation upon the accession of Edward I in 1272. A few years before, at the time of the Barons' War, there had been indications that the magnates might take over the government as an efficient ruling class. It had looked as if the monarchy would be limited by the full power of the common council to provide and affirm law. Events proved that impossible, and the failure of the baronial reformers went far to discredit such a view. Lack of solidarity and personal selfishness within the ranks of the barons was fatal to the maintenance of their authority. Moreover, persistent ideas about a monarchy which, it was thought, could not be limited "by any power or authority whatsoever" were significantly responsible for the renewed prestige of the kingship after

[4] Jolliffe, *Constitutional History*, p. 335.
[5] *Ibid.*

Henry's victory at Evesham. The magnates in parliament, as it turned out, never recovered the position to which they had laid claim at the time of the Barons' War, that they were feudal councilors whom the king should consult on important affairs of the kingdom. Feudalism, in other words, was ceasing to be that general standard by which the validity of institutions was judged. "It is yielding to monarchical empiricism," to ideas about community, and to economic realism.[6]

The future was in the hands of Henry's son, Edward I. The course and the development of English institutions was so profoundly molded by his handiwork that it may fairly be said that he was one of England's greatest kings. For the first time since the beginning of the baronial reform in 1258, "the country found a leader more single-minded than de Montfort, and one whose instinct in what he felt to be essential for the good of the country chimed more exactly with its own than that of any king since the Conquest."[7] A period of important legislative activity, Edward's reign is marked by that great series of statutes which were to form the nucleus of the Statute Book—famous enactments which systematized the land-law and the courts, and hardened every practice of the administration. Everywhere the franchises and the immunities of feudal jurisdictions were questioned, for the purpose of defining them with a view to insisting that they were held as a privilege in return for a corresponding obligation.[8] The entire machinery of government was vastly elaborated, and its efficiency extended; lawyers, experts, and foreign jurists flocked to Westminster.

Edward understood the desirability, for his purposes, of continuing the regular meetings of parliament which, as has been pointed out, had become an established practice during the later years of Henry III. But parliament became under

6 *Ibid.*, p. 331.
7 *Ibid.*, p. 333.
8 Cf. *Select Cases Before the Court of King's Bench* (ed. Sayles, Selden Society: London, 1938), ii. liv-lviii.

Edward, more than ever before, the time when the entire administrative machine was brought into sharp focus. Parliament under Edward I becomes the term for much legal business, "the term to which lands are to be replevied or until which a wardship may be retained, the term upon which payments of various kinds are to be made or until which they are respited, the term until which taxation may be suspended."[9] It is the time for submitting inquisitions and returns of various kinds, or for the rendering of homage. Those who attend the king's parliament come as the servants or petitioners of the crown, not its advisers. The records which have come down to us indicate very clearly that the core and essence of the Edwardian parliaments was the king's small, permanent, inner council. If parliament under Edward I is at all a definite thing, it is more in the nature of a court of justice than a legislative or consultative assembly. The rudimentary legislative functions which the magnates were beginning to exercise in the 1250's were seriously curtailed: even their consent was hardly regarded as essential to the validity of an enactment. The judges and the experts of the inner council framed statutes and considered the advisability of enactments. They were the "lions under the throne," and what they did was done chiefly with the authority of the king's prerogative. "No peer has the king in the realm," writes Bracton, and it is literally true.[10]

In the administration of government in the last quarter of the thirteenth century we can see that definition and differentiation have superseded the general and unsystematized work of the great council of an earlier day. Some consultation between the magnates and the council might take place in parliament, but if the practices of the previous reign lingered on, they were adapted to the king's ideas about his own prerogative. Magnates were summoned to several of the

[9] H. G. Richardson and G. O. Sayles, *Bulletin of the Institute of Historical Research* (1929), vi. 71.
[10] Bracton, *De Legibus* (ed. Woodbine), ii. 33.

parliaments in Edward's reign, and with increasing frequency towards the end. They were called to treat with the king on various matters to be put before them by the king and council. Generally the writs specify what that business is to be: Gascon affairs,[11] the fulfillment of the promise of an aid,[12] the establishment of a form of government for Scotland.[13] But the magnates who are summoned are differently selected on each occasion according to whom the king wants for the matter at hand. As a class the baronage no longer has an official standing. Parliament was clearly "not dominated by amateur administrators and amateur jurists, by barons, knights, and burgesses."[14] An efficient civil service replaced the half-casual administration of three generations before. If lip-service was still paid to ideas about counsel and consent, it was because the king thought it expedient. Nevertheless, the persistence of such ideas is not without significance. Statutes enacted in parliament were frequently said to be done with the assent of the magnates and the community of the realm there present. Representatives were said to be summoned because the king's business could not be accomplished without them. And in the grandly eloquent clause inserted in one of the summonses to parliament in 1295, and reminiscent of a sentence in the imperial *Code* of Justinian,[15] Edward pronounced: "A most just law, established by the careful providence of sacred princes, exhorts and decrees that what touches all should be approved of all"—*quod omnes tangit, ab omnibus approbetur.*[16]

Phrases of that kind which may greet us in the preamble of a statute or in the opening clause of a writ were by no means wholly sham. They crystallized familiar principles of consent

11 *Parliamentary Writs*, i. 78.
12 *Ibid.*, i. 47.
13 *Ibid.*, i. 136.
14 H. G. Richardson and G. O. Sayles, *English Historical Review* (1931). xlvi. 550.
15 *Code*, 5. 59. 5: "ut quod omnes similiter tangit, ab omnibus comprobetur."
16 *Parliamentary Writs*, i. 30. This sentence of the writ is discussed by G. L. Haskins, "Representation and Consent," *Notes and Queries* (1937), clxxii. 258-259.

in the procedure of the courts of law, wherein all parties whose rights were in question must be summoned to appear.[17] Moreover, those phrases propagandized what were to the crown very important concepts—general ideas about coöperation, about the king as the fountain of justice, as the greatest power and authority in the kingdom. Such considerations, however, together with the increasing frequency of summonses of representatives, the inclusion of proctors of the parochial clergy, the opening of parliament to poor suitors who could not afford costly procedure in the regular courts—all these must not obscure the real function of parliament in the time of Edward I. Parliament was simply the efficient vehicle of the king's prerogative. If some other institution had proved equally adaptable, equally suitable to serve the same ends, Edward would have used that instead.

For all the strength of the king and his new administration, the relics of the old system did not die or disappear all at once. Independence, criticism, and distrust continued. It characterized, indeed, the history of the next hundred years, the reigns of the first three Edwards. Discord and deadlocks were constant, typified by the well-known account of the Earl of Norfolk's defying Edward I over the question of serving in the army abroad. "By God, earl," swore the king, "you shall either go or hang." "By God, O king," retorted Norfolk, "I will neither go nor hang."[18]

The hundred years following the accession of Edward I are concerned to a great extent with searching for a workable substitute to replace the feudal arrangements which had gone. For the future, it was a period of importance, because the workable balance which was finally struck at the end of Edward III's reign was a form of parliamentary monarchy. To a degree that could hardly have been foretold from the character of his grandfather's reign, the question of authority

<hr>

[17] See G. Post, "A Romano-Canonical Maxim, 'Quod Omnes Tangit,' in Bracton," *Traditio* (1946), iv. 197, especially 227, 249.
[18] Stubbs, *Constitutional History*, ii. 138.

was settled in the constitutional coöperation of the king and the lords on one side, and the commons on the other.

It is only from the standpoint of the modern age that "the feeble beginnings of popular representation have any importance in parliamentary history."[19] It must be understood that, in the reigns of Edward I and Edward II, representatives of the commons were not in any way essential to a properly constituted parliament. Neither taxation nor legislation was the normal business of parliament. Parliament was first of all a meeting of the king and his council for judicial purposes. Insofar as it was a general *colloquium,* it was a meeting to which a very large number of groups might be asked to come, in order to learn the intentions of the king with respect to such matters as war or taxation. In the early fourteenth century, moreover, parliament was not a body of fixed composition; it was nothing that might be called an institution. Barons, earls, bishops, archdeacons, proctors of the lower clergy, knights, burgesses, groups of lawyers or merchants— any or all of these might receive summonses to parliament. It is important to note that those same groups, or any one of them, might be called to a central assembly which was not a parliament. In the time of Edward I there are many instances of *colloquia* of magnates, or of merchants, or of knights and burgesses, called for deliberative purposes, from which the legal business which characterized a parliament was almost wholly absent.[20] It was in such assemblies, rather than in parliament, that various groups might be asked to give the king advice or to give support to policies which he had initiated.

Towards the end of the reign, however, certain combinations of elements in parliament began to recur more frequently than others. Those were the barons, the clergy, the knights, and the burgesses. Those groups became the recog-

[19] H. G. Richardson, *Transactions of the Royal Historical Society,* 4th ser. (1928), xi. 168.
[20] For example, *Parliamentary Writs,* i. 21, 26, 164; Stubbs, *Select Charters,* p. 496.

nized elements which afforced a meeting of parliament, and Edward found it to his advantage to treat with them on certain matters which earlier in his reign he had discussed in non-parliamentary assemblies. The latter were by no means eliminated by the new expedient, but in the course of the next two reigns many issues involving advice and consultation were drawn within the sphere of parliamentary business. It was thus that financial and consultative matters came increasingly to be associated with the work of parliament.

In speaking of the groups which were normally summoned to parliament, it must be remembered that other groups, such as the merchants, were called and at times seemed on the point of becoming permanent elements in parliament.[21] The king's need of money frequently led him to summon any class which might contribute to the ever-empty treasury. The habits of the thirteenth century, however, were against such special summonses, and the long political training of the knights and burgesses helped to account for the disappearance from parliament of groups other than the magnates, the clergy, the knights, and the burgesses. The practices of Henry III's reign had toughened the representative quality of the knights and burgesses, and had developed a tradition of their speaking with the authority of their communities. The tide, therefore, was strong and persistent in the direction of approaching the basic political units of the country—the county and the borough—through their accustomed representatives.

The writs by which the representatives were summoned to parliament ordered them to appear with full power to bind themselves and their communities. What was done in parliament the communities were expected to accept as "valid and agreed." In the early fourteenth century their representatives were summoned only to hear and consent to what was to be decided by others. In spite of their numbers—generally between sixty and seventy knights and some two hundred bur-

---

[21] As late as 1406 the king's judicial officers seem to be regarded as an "estate" of parliament. See *Rotuli Parliamentorum*, iii. 579.

gesses were present at a parliament—the "hearing" involved listening to the purpose for which the king needed money. The "consenting" usually involved acceding to the king's needs.

Attendance at parliament was, like attendance at the borough court or the shire court, clearly in the nature of an obligation. Not only was the knight or burgess not anxious to make a weary and frequently dangerous journey to Westminster to attend to affairs which for the most part were of little interest to him, but the shires and boroughs themselves were anxious to evade the duty of sending up representatives. The communities had to pay the expenses of its representatives—the knights at the rate of four shillings a day, the burgesses at two shillings

Attempts at evasion of the parliamentary summons were frequent, so that the king demanded sureties for an elected member. Either a number of men made themselves his pledges, or some of his chattels were "bound over" by the sheriff until the session was over.[22] Frequently the boroughs ignored the summons;[23] others were sometimes able to purchase exemption by pleading unusual expenses, as the building of new walls or the repairing of a bridge.[24] In the reign of Edward III one town even complained that the duty of sending representatives had been imposed maliciously.[25] Clearly to talk about the *right* of membership in the king's parliament would be to misunderstand entirely the nature of the assembly.

At first sight it may appear curious that the commons ever attained any degree of influence, if the foregoing description of their position is accurate, and if their reluctance to obey the summons was so marked. In the first place, however, the fact that they were a persistent element in the administration,

---

22 *Parliamentary Writs*, i. 22: "districti sunt per omnia bona et catalla sua quod sint ad diem, etc." Cf. also, *ibid.*, i. 66: "districtus est per octo boves et quatuor afros."
23 *Parliamentary Writs*, i. 72, 121, 123.
24 *Rotuli Parliamentorum*, iii. 395.
25 *Ibid.*, ii. 459.

that as time went on they were regularly summoned to parliament, is a matter of first importance. Their regular presence ultimately ensured their becoming an indispensable part of the institution. In the second place, since their constituencies were obliged to pay the representatives, the counties and towns were anxious that some sort of effective work should be done, or at least that some show of resistance should be put up. That fact seems to have furthered the growth of political responsibility among the commons, and hence to have ensured their more active participation in the work of parliament.[26] Moreover, we know that in the fourteenth century some towns sent instructions to their members during the course of a session and asked for reports on what had taken place when the representatives returned.[27] In the third place, the principle that the consent of the representatives was necessary to any grants of money had been recognized at an early date. In the so-called statute *De Tallagio non Concedendo,* in 1297, it is stated in the first article: "No tallage or aid shall be laid or levied by us or our heirs in our realm, without the good will and assent of the archbishops, bishops, and other prelates, earls, barons, knights, burgesses, and other freemen of our realm."[28]

In the fourteenth century it became an established practice that assent to taxation was something that was given in parliament by those who paid the tax. It was by enforcing that principle by a hint of resistance that the representatives were able to give consent some meaning of control. Now and again Edward I attempted to secure grants from non-parlia-

---

[26] Evidence of a feeling of responsibility of representatives towards their "constituencies" can be found in a passage in *Richard the Redeless:* "We are sent from the shires to make known their grievances, to discuss matters on their behalf and to stick to that, and only make grants of their money to the great men in a regular way, unless there is war. If we are false to the people who pay our wages, we are not earning them." Cam, *Liberties and Communities of Medieval England,* p. 230.

[27] See H. G. Richardson and G. O. Sayles, *English Historical Review* (1938), liii. 436-37; *Rotuli Parliamentorum Hactenus Inediti* (ed. Richardson and Sayles, Camden Society: London, 1935), p. 100.

[28] Stubbs, *Select Charters,* p. 493.

mentary *ad hoc* assemblies of merchants or townsfolk, or even by local negotiations throughout the country. But such attempts were never successful. If they had been, as they were in France under Philip the Fair, concerted resistance would have been impossible. In 1282, for example, Edward sent out Sir John de Kirkby with letters recommending him to all sheriffs, mayors, and bailiffs of England. He was authorized to report on the "response and will" of those concerned with regard to an aid the king proposed to ask.[29] Kirkby was coldly received; and although similar measures were again attempted fifteen years later, Edward found that it was in parliament alone that he could expect what he considered a reasonable response. That fact assured the magnates, as well as the knights and burgesses, permanent membership in parliament. Equally important was the growing idea of the counties and boroughs as fiscal and political units, a notion which was firmly established by 1300. Somewhat earlier, as has been pointed out, the crown had begun to deal with those communities through their representatives, in order to circumvent the feudal chain of command. That practice further helped to block the way to negotiation with individuals and groups outside of parliament.

Concerted resistance showed itself in parliament as early as 1290, when the grant of an aid by the barons and knights was made conditional on the expulsion of all the Jews from England.[30] The fulfillment of that condition netted the crown the largest amount ever achieved by a single tax in the Middle Ages. In 1297, and again in 1301, aids were granted on condition that the king republish the Great Charter and the Charter of the Forest.[31] As a result of such stipulations, political issues came to be dependent in some measure upon the consent to aids in parliament. In time, the redress of grievances

29 *Ibid.*, pp. 456-57.
30 *Annales Monastici*, iii. 362.
31 *Chronicon Walteri de Hemingburgh*, ii. 138; *Parliamentary Writs*, i. 104-105.

became a frequent condition precedent to the granting of customs and taxes.

The importance of that fact is of especial significance because it became increasingly clear in the fourteenth century that the government could not "live of its own." Taxes in the fourteenth century were roughly of two sorts. There was the gracious aid, which was levied on personal property, that is, on movables, such as cattle, grain, and personal effects. Then there were the customs, levied on wool, leather, wine, and like commodities. The gracious aids, from the time they had first been asked for in the early thirteenth century, had come to require the consent of those who were to pay the tax. It was otherwise with the customs. As early as 1275, parliament granted the king what was known as the ancient custom, a fixed tax on wine, wool, and leather.[32] But the crown's need of money tempted the king constantly to enlarge the scope of the commodities covered. The extension was achieved either by wholesale seizures, or by extra-parliamentary grants made by the merchants. But the net result of the policy was to excite the opposition of the commons. In 1309 they pointed out in a petition that the incidence of these taxes fell not on the merchants but on the consumers.[33]

A series of similar complaints intensified the issue; it resulted in eliminating the merchants as a possible estate in parliament, and in preventing the king from allying himself with them in order to tax the body of the nation at his discretion. In 1340 a statute was enacted containing the clause that the nation should be no more "charged nor grieved to make common Aid, or to sustain Charge, if it be not by the common assent of the Prelates, Earls, Barons, and other great Men, and Commons of our said Realm of England, and that in the Parliament."[34] Edward III affirmed the provision in 1377,

[32] *Parliamentary Writs,* i. 2.
[33] *Rotuli Parliamentorum,* i. 443.
[34] *Statutes of the Realm,* i. 290.

promising that only extreme necessity would force him to disregard it. Thus the control of the customs, as well as the gracious aids, came under the view of parliament. No further attempt at unauthorized taxation of merchandise was made again in the Middle Ages.[35]

The technicalities of revenue, it has been said, "would not be of great interest were they not part of the process by which the various elements, public, private, feudal, and sovereign, of the king's power were being brought into a single concept of royal authority exercised under the criticism of parliament."[36] The struggle for the control of taxes and customs helped to give the commons unity and threw them into prominence as an estate in parliament. Moreover, as a result of their occasional insistence that supply and redress of grievances went hand in hand, political business and discussion began to intrude into parliament. In that discussion the commons began to participate and to have a certain influence on legislation.

The prestige of the representatives was further enhanced by the civil disorders of Edward II's reign. Soon after the death of Edward I, the growing resentment of the baronage against his policies and administration came to a head. Opposition to the wastefulness and the incompetence of his son produced in 1309 a situation similar to the baronial crisis of 1258. Again the kingship was put in the hands of a committee of barons appointed to reform the administration, and again the barons turned for support to the less prominent element in society, the knights and burgesses. In 1309 the articles of a common petition drawn up by the representatives, which complained of royal encroachments and the improper hearing of pleas, was embodied in a statute enacted by the parliament of Stamford.[37] The same thing happened again in

---

[35] Stubbs, *Constitutional History*, ii. 558.
[36] Jolliffe, *Constitutional History*, p. 404.
[37] *Rotuli Parliamentorum*, i. 443-45; *Statutes of the Realm*, i. 154-56.

1320.[38] Previously, little attention had been paid by the council to petitions of the knights and burgesses.

Those precedents were of considerable importance, for up to this time statutes had been devised and framed almost entirely by the royal judges and experts of the council. Moreover, it was thought that changes in the law were a function of the king's prerogative and should come from above. The reign of Edward II distinctly raised the prestige of the commons in that regard, and by the opening of the reign of Edward III, five years later, "the typical legislative enactment becomes one based upon a petition of the *commune* which in a special way is represented by the commons."[39] The increased importance of the representatives was also expressly recognized by Edward II when he regained power in 1322. In the Statute of York, enacted in that year, it was proclaimed that matters to be established for the estate of the realm and of the people "shall be treated, accorded and established in Parliaments, by our Lord the King, and by the Assent of the Prelates, Earls, Barons, and the Commonalty of the Realm; according as it hath been heretofore accustomed."[40] The meaning of this clause of the statute has given rise to considerable discussion.[41] That it did not mean, as Stubbs thought, that the full coöperation of all the estates in parliament was "necessary for the establishment of any measure touching the king and the realm,"[42] is clear from what we know of the nature of parliament at that time. But whatever the matters were which were to be treated in parliament as had been theretofore accustomed, it is significant that the position of the knights and burgesses (now the "commonalty of the realm") in parliament was so expressly recognized.

[38] *Statutes of the Realm,* i. 180. Cf. H. L. Gray, *The Influence of the Commons on Early Legislation* (Cambridge, Mass., 1932), p. 214, note 17.
[39] H. G. Richardson and G. O. Sayles, *Law Quarterly Review* (1934), 1. 569.
[40] *Statutes of the Realm,* i. 189.
[41] Haskins, *The Statute of York.* See also J. R. Strayer, *American Historical Review* (1941), xlvii. 1; G. Lapsley, *English Historical Review* (1941), lvi. 22, 411.
[42] Stubbs, *Constitutional History,* ii. 628.

When the commons are found to be participating actively in enactment, as well as in finance, it may be said that their position is assured and that their political power has begun. In the reign of Edward I, it had been customary to dismiss the representatives as soon as they had granted an aid. In fact, the knights were sometimes dismissed on the same day they arrived. Only those who had some special business at parliament were invited to remain. In 1290, the knights were not summoned to parliament until the main work of the session—the drafting of the Statute of *Quia Emptores*—had been completed. By the time of Edward III, when the commons are almost invariably summoned to parliament, they remain throughout most of the session. Many knights and burgesses represent the same constituencies at more than one parliament. Chaucer says of his Franklin, "ful ofte tyme he was knyght of the shire."[43] Often as many as thirty or forty knights in a parliament of Edward III's reign had had previous parliamentary experience. There are instances of the same members having been reëlected to as many as eighteen different parliaments; six or eight is entirely usual.[44] Experience of that kind unquestionably helped to form traditions and opinion in the nascent house of commons.

Nevertheless it is still, even in the reign of Edward III, too early to speak of the house of commons as such. Although the various groups might deliberate separately, parliament was still unicameral. It was a large meeting of many people in the presence of the king and his council. That characteristic was long maintained. Not, indeed, until the reign of Henry VIII do we hear of a house of lords. Not until well on in the fifteenth century do we find a reference to a *domus communis*, or "common house."[45]

It was not possible for the knights and burgesses to act in a

43 G. Chaucer, *Complete Works* (ed. Robinson: Cambridge, Mass. 1933), p. 23.
44 K. Wood-Legh, "The Knights' Attendance in the Parliaments of Edward III," *English Historical Review* (1932), xlvii. 398.
45 *Rotuli Parliamentorum*, iv. 422; v. 177.

joint capacity, representing the whole community of the realm instead of their several constituencies, until a *rapprochement* between the two elements had first been effected. In the early fourteenth century that would hardly have seemed possible. Attached to the barons by similar interests, often by ties of blood, the knights naturally sided with the magnates, leaving the burgesses by themselves. The gulf between the two sections of the elected representatives was wide. Moreover, unlike the knights, the borough representatives were seldom called upon to take part in any of the administrative work of parliament. Furthermore, in the beginning the magnates and the knights granted the same tax to the king, whereas the burgesses made a separate grant. In 1306, for example, the knights and magnates together voted the king a tax of a thirtieth on their movables, the burgesses a twentieth.[46]

As much as anything, it was the civil wars of Edward II's reign which forced the magnates and the knights apart. As a stable and on the whole conservative element in society, the knights saw that the royal government was far more permanent and efficient than the self-appointed committees of barons, racked by bitter feuds and personal greed. Then, too, a distinction between the magnates and the representatives had been emphasized by a difference in the wording of the writs by which they were summoned.[47] Moreover, the magnates, following the lead of the clergy, began to insist on private consultation within parliament, and that claim fostered the principle of separate orders.[48] However, the actual coalescence of the knights and burgesses is one of the obscure social and political facts of the fourteenth century. No doubt their joint procuratorial character, their joint and common

---

46 R. Brady, *An Historical Treatise of Cities and Boroughs* (London, 1777), Appendix, pp. 26-29.

47 The magnates were usually summoned "ad colloquium et tractatum de quibusdam arduis negotiis que regnum Anglie tangunt," whereas the knights and burgesses (at least until 1313) were summoned "ad audiendum et faciendum quod tunc de communi consilio ordinabitur."

48 Jolliffe. *Constitutional History,* pp. 375-76.

training in the borough court and the county court, supplied strong bonds. Again, the social ties between the knights and burgesses grew closer as the gulf between the landed gentry and a baronage on its way to becoming a peerage necessarily widened.[49] The younger sons of the county knight often sought wives, occupations, or estates in the towns; more than one son of an impoverished knightly family was not above marrying the daughter of a rich burgess. Chiefly, however, common deliberation between the town and county representatives was provoked by the king, who insisted on a corporate response to his demands for money. It is important to note that whenever a grant was made conditionally, the knights and burgesses are mentioned separately from the magnates. In general, it is fair to say that their joint activity was sponsored from the outside rather than from within their own groups.

The beginnings of joint consultation between the knights and burgesses meant necessarily that they deliberated apart from the clergy and magnates, outside of parliament. Shortly after the accession of Edward III, they adopted the practice of retiring to the Painted Chamber in the Palace to deliberate secretly and apart.[50] Later the Chapter House of Westminster Abbey became "the ancient place" of the commons.[51] After reaching their decision, they would return again to parliament. As early as 1332 we have clear evidence of their acting in this way, and consulting together on subsidies and their petition of grievances.[52] The lead in discussion was taken by the knights, whose experience and training in administrative work particularly fitted them for that role. Their wealth and social prestige, too, unquestionably helped to give them a dominant position in the commons.

The records of the commons in parliament reveal so many

49 It was in the reign of Edward II that the conception of peerage took shape. See H. G. Richardson, *Transactions of the Royal Historical Society,* 4th ser. (1946), xxviii. 26, note 1.
50 *Rotuli Parliamentorum,* ii. 136.
51 *Ibid.,* ii. 237, 322.
52 *Ibid.,* ii. 66.

conflicting tendencies that it is practically impossible to say with exactness what power they attained during the course of the fourteenth century. The large number of petitions running in the name of the commons has frequently been taken as a basis for presuming extensive and varied activities. But close scrutiny shows that the commons had no secretariat, no official committees, not even any records of their discussions. There are frequent duplications in the articles of their petitions, and the petitions themselves are often repetitive.[53] There was apparently no guarantee that all the representatives attending parliament, or even a majority of them, are meant by the phrase "the commons of the realm" at the head of a petition. The commons often adopted as their own the petitions of others,[54] and people who had very little right to do so frequently took it upon themselves to present petitions in the name of the commons. "No effective rules had yet been devised which would prevent any man or group of people from representing that they were voicing a national demand."[55] Yet during the reign of Edward III, the commons became the normal channel through which petitions passed. By the end of the century they had become an integral part of the machinery of government.

On matters of government policy, the commons in the fourteenth century generally acquiesced in decisions made by the king and the magnates. Despite their right to withhold financial aid, they did not use it as a means to secure control in government or in foreign affairs. Even the formulation of policies which entailed expenditures "were above the heads of the commons and, to all seeming, above their desires."[56]

53 D. Rayner, "The Forms and Machinery of the 'Commune Petition' in the Fourteenth Century," *English Historical Review* (1941), lvi. 198, 549.
54 For example, a petition of merchants in 1372. H. G. Richardson, *Transactions of the Royal Historical Society*, 4th ser. (1946), xxviii. 34, note 1. Cf. also *Rotuli Parliamentorum*, iii. 525-26, 583.
55 H. G. Richardson and G. O. Sayles, *Bulletin of the Institute of Historical Research* (1931), ix. 9. See also G. L. Haskins, "Three Early Petitions of the Commonalty," *Speculum* (1937), xii. 314.
56 H. G. Richardson, *Transactions of the Royal Historical Society*, 4th ser. (1946), xxviii. 29.

They disclaimed responsibility when consulted about the expedition to Flanders in 1383.[57] On the heresy legislation of 1382 and 1401 they took an ineffectual stand.[58] If they played more of a part in the impeachment of Latimer in 1376, they took no part in the labor legislation of 1349 and 1351.[59] But, as Mr. Richardson points out, "they were not expected to make any great contribution to statecraft."[60] A record of 1399 states that, besides consenting to grants and objecting to excessive taxation, it was the function of the commons to present the grievances of the people and to sue for suitable remedies.[61] For the decision of matters of policy their presence was not required.

Such rules of procedure as the commons had in the fourteenth century appear to have been dictated by the circumstances of the moment. In a recently discovered chronicle, written towards the end of the fourteenth century, we have an extensive account of the Good Parliament of 1376, presumably from an eyewitness.[62] The commons appear as an unorganized body which debates without rules in the Chapter House of the Abbey. All the speech-making is done by the knights, who speak at will from the "lectron" on whatever matters they feel should be brought to the attention of the other representatives. The debates continue, off and on, for something like ten days. On the eve of proceeding to the king they choose a speaker, who acts not as chairman, but as a member who reports to the king the wishes of the commons and the results of their consultation. How long before that time it was customary to elect a speaker, we do not know; probably as early as 1343. In any case, the desirability of having someone act as a mouthpiece of the commons doubt-

---

[57] *Rotuli Parliamentorum*, iii. 145-48.
[58] H. G. Richardson, *Transactions of the Royal Historical Society*, 4th ser. (1946), xxviii. 31.
[59] *Ibid.*
[60] *Ibid.*, p. 32.
[61] *Rotuli Parliamentorum*, iii. 420.
[62] *The Anonimalle Chronicle, 1333-1381* (ed. Galbraith: Manchester, 1927), pp. 79-94.

less gave rise to the practice. If so, the original suggestion may well have come from the king. On the other hand, the dangers of reporting some of the commons' decisions were considerable. We find that the speaker's duty is to anticipate any slander or insult to the king's dignity by asking leave to report criticism without offense.[63] Some historians, searching for early instances of the commons' power, have seen in the speaker's protestation the concern of the commons to safeguard a right to free speech. The true implication of the speaker's apology is that if the commons' decisions were displeasing to the king, they were liable to punishment.[64] Their concern, therefore, was to anticipate his possible irritation by an apology in advance. The apology is a further illustration of the inferior position of the commons in parliament.

When it is alleged that the king's ministers in the fourteenth century became answerable to the commons for their acts,[65] it must again be insisted that a modern conception of ministerial responsibility is being read back into an age which knew no such idea. Latimer, Neville, Michael de la Pole, and others, it is true, were called before parliament to answer for their misdeeds. But the prosecutions were in large measure instigated by the lords appellant, who prompted the commons to initiate the proceedings. If the indictments are significant in the development of the powers of the house of commons, it is not because they illustrate the power which the commons had attained by the end of the fourteenth century, but because they illustrate the importance of the commons' petitions in parliamentary business. However, the impeachment proceedings emphasize that, although the commons were the initiating organ in parliament at least in form, they seldom exercised effective control. As petitioners before

---

63 Cf. *Rotuli Parliamentorum*, iii. 34-35.
64 *Ibid.*, iii. 73, 357.
65 Stubbs, *Constitutional History*, ii. 593: "The condemnation of Michael de la Pole especially showed that the great officers of state must henceforth regard themselves as responsible to the nation."

the king's highest court, they were critics rather than formulators of policy.

Yet the very fact that they presented frequent joint petitions, which voiced the grievances of the country, was highly important for the development of the house of commons. Petitions, presented and answered in parliament, provided an alternative to prolonged discontent and possible civil war. Even though the king and council had the power to reject the commons' petitions in whole or in part, such parts as were unobjectionable were habitually accepted and embodied in statutes, which had come to be accepted as the highest kind of law. By 1399, and thereafter for half a century, most statutes were enacted on the basis of petitions of the commons.[66] As Mr. Jolliffe says, "It is to the reigns of the three Edwards that we owe the creation of parliament, and the peaceful and almost unnoticed growth of its most essential principles."[67]

[66] Gray, *The Influence of the Commons*, p. 414.
[67] Jolliffe, *Constitutional History*, p. 405.

THE HIGHEST AND MOST AUTHENTICAL
COURT OF ENGLAND

For three hundred years parliament has been the supreme legislating organ of England, and the house of commons has been its most important constituent part. From as early as the opening of the fourteenth century, it is possible to trace the faint beginnings of the power which was later to be acquired by the commons. The control of the representatives of the counties and towns over taxation was achieved as a practical matter by the end of the thirteenth century, and their continued appearance in parliament was assured by the king's acceptance of the principle that no tax could be levied without their consent. Control over duties and customs followed, and in 1340 it was enacted that the nation should be no more "charged nor grieved to make common Aid, or to sustain Charge, if it be not by the common assent of the Prelates, Earls, Barons, and other great Men, and Commons of our said Realm of England, and that in the Parliament."[1] The control of the commons over finance was followed by a certain influence in politics, diplomacy, and enactments. Moreover, resistance to taxation was frequently used as a lever to force the king to redress grievances laid before him by petition. By the end of the fourteenth century it may be said that changes in the law were effected largely through petitions presented by the commons in parliament.

Present-day interest in representative government and the legislative sovereignty of the people has tended to focus attention too much on the commons and on their winning of the initiative. Likewise, over-zealous occupation with the origins of the house of commons has tended to obscure what was in the Middle Ages the real nature of parliament. When

[1] *Statutes of the Realm*, i. 290.

Sir Thomas Smith, writing in the time of Queen Elizabeth, spoke of parliament as "the highest and most authenticall court of Englande,"[2] he was using no archaic phrase of euphuistic rhetoric. He was speaking of parliament as it had been regarded throughout the Middle Ages and as many of his contemporaries still regarded it, that is, as essentially the highest court of justice in the kingdom.

The fact that parliament throughout most of the Middle Ages was first and foremost a court of justice may at first sight appear curious. The fact that diplomacy, political business, the granting of taxes, changes in the law were all discussed in parliament suggests that a good deal of what is now the business of a legislature was the business of a medieval parliament both in England and in other countries. The growing political importance of the elected representatives tends to throw what we today call the non-judicial activities in which they participated into higher relief. But it must never be forgotten that parliament was in essence an expanded session of the king's council. Although new elements were grafted on to the old, the old did not die out but continued along with the new. It is impossible properly to understand the growth of the commons, whether we speak of control acquired or initiative won, without taking account of what was for nearly four hundred years the most prominent characteristic of parliament. Its character even in the late fourteenth century was essentially that of the king's court, and judicial business formed the nucleus of its proceedings.

To the proper performance of the functions of parliament —to its legal competence and its authority—the presence or absence of the commons and most of the magnates was immaterial. It was only because the commons were regular and frequent petitioners before the king's court that they ultimately acquired the importance which they did.

The financial needs of the crown first prompted the regular summoning of shire and town representatives. The redress

[2] T. Smith, *De Republica Anglorum* (ed. Alston: Cambridge, 1906), p. 58.

of grievances was frequently bought in return for supply. But that redress was secured by joint petitions of the commons, directed to the king, who held his court before parliament. The hearing of petitions by the king in council was essentially a judicial proceeding to which the commons were party. Moreover, other functions of the representatives were also regarded as judicial in nature; and it may be said that their obligation to attend parliament was founded in great part on the notion that they, like the prelates, earls, and barons, were regarded as suitors at the king's court. The first knights of the shire who were summoned to appear before the council were called to defend the judgment of their county or to bear the record of a case from the county court. The writs of 1275 directed the sheriff to see that the knights who were elected should be expert in the law, *de discretioribus in lege militibus*.[3] The judicial aspect of their functions persisted until at least the seventeenth century and can be seen with exceptional clearness in *Fitzharris's Case*, in which the commons are referred to as the "greatest and wisest inquest in England."[4]

Whatever prominence in parliament the commons may have achieved in the Middle Ages, their position was always subordinate to the king and council. Important as we, today, may regard the representative features of the house of commons, it is their judicial character which explains not only their position in parliament but the nature of the power which they acquired in the Middle Ages. This chapter is concerned with explaining the nature of parliament as a court and with showing the bearing of that fact on the growth of representative government.

The earliest definition of parliament which we have comes from the thirteenth-century lawyer known as Fleta. Writing

3 Stubbs, *Select Charters*, p. 442.
4 8 *Cobbett State Trials* 286.

in or about the year 1290, he says: "The king has his court in his council in his parliament, in the presence of prelates, earls, barons, nobles and other learned men, where judicial doubts are determined, and new remedies are established for new wrongs, and justice is done to each according to his deserts."[5] Fleta's "council-in-parliament" was the judicial phase of the king's small, permanent council, which had taken shape in the reign of Henry III. By the reign of Edward I the judicial work of the council—in particular, the hearing and despatching of petitions—had become so great that such work was concentrated in special sessions. Thereafter, those sessions "appear as a sharply distinguished organ of the state of extreme importance under a name which they share with the *colloquia* of the magnates—Parliament."[6] When it met, it was a large body, including the king's principal officials and the judges of all the great courts.[7] It was a court set over other courts and the highest in the realm. The business which came before it was of a kind which would normally come before a court. That business was largely judicial, concerned with cases of first instance, cases on appeal, cases that had proved too novel or too difficult for judges in the inferior courts.

Whenever we are told what the people at large expect of parliament, it is a variation on the theme of giving justice to all. Despite the increased proportion of parliamentary time taken up in the fourteenth century with diplomacy, war and taxation, "the dispensation of justice remained in the eyes of the people . . . the prime purpose of parliament."[8] The writ which summoned the commons to parliament in 1348 explains that the king's purpose is not to ask for aids or

---

5 *Fleta*, p. 66.

6 Jolliffe, *Constitutional History*, p. 339.

7 *Records of the Parliament of 1305*, pp. xlii-xliii. See also Pollock and Maitland, *History of English Law*, i. 200: "For judicial purposes the parliamentary sessions of the council can be conceived as strengthened, as 'afforced,' sessions of the king's bench."

8 H. G. Richardson and G. O. Sayles, *Bulletin of the Institute of Historical Research* (1931), ix. 2.

tallages from the people, or to impose other burdens, but it
is to do justice to the people of the realm in respect to their
complaints and grievances.[9] In 1362 and in 1376 the commons ask for annual parliaments, in order that divers grievances and mischiefs arising from day to day may be redressed,
or that errors and falsities found in the realm may be corrected.[10] In a petition which the commons present in Richard II's first parliament it is stated that only in parliament
can suits be determined which are delayed in the king's
courts. It is only in parliament, they allege, that judgment
can be given when the justices are divided in opinion; it is
only to parliament that men may come when aggrieved by
the king's ministers; it is in parliament that petitions are
presented and determined.[11]

Such was the character of parliament in the time of Edward
III; such it had been in the time of his father and grandfather.
In the Lenten parliament of 1305, we find Henry de Aynes-
ham, a mason, suing for the recovery of wages due in connection with work done at the king's castle at Carnarvon.[12]
John de Crofton asks to be allowed a new writ for recovery
which was not granted by the chancery.[13] William de White-
well complains of abuses in the course of justice and asks the
king to do right.[14] Such cases are typical. They justify the
statement that when every nonessential has been stripped
away, the essence of parliament is "the dispensing of justice
by the king or by someone who in a very special sense represents the king."[15]

It follows that the early history of parliament will be to
a great extent the history of a court, of a court set over other
courts and designed to dispense a higher justice. In having

9 *Lords' Reports on the Dignity of a Peer*, iv. 573.
10 *Rotuli Parliamentorum*, ii. 271, 355.
11 *Ibid.*, iii. 23.
12 *Records of the Parliament of 1305*, p. 87, number 147.
13 *Ibid.*, pp. 158-59, number 251.
14 *Ibid.*, p. 166, number 266.
15 H. G. Richardson and G. O. Sayles, *Bulletin of the Institute of Historical Research* (1928), v. 133.

to use the word "court" we are unfortunately at a disadvantage. The word throws the judicial aspects of parliament into too sharp relief. This statement may seem paradoxical after what has just been said. But the truth is that predominant as were the judicial functions of parliament in the opening years of the fourteenth century other functions came to be included in parliamentary business. Those new functions were not distinguished as being non-judicial; on the contrary, they were thought to be the proper business of the king's highest court. Hence, when we speak of the jurisdiction of parliament as being primarily the administration of justice, much more is meant than the mere administration of justice as we know it today in our own courts.

In the sense applicable to parliament, the word "court" is difficult to define in modern terms. Today we think of a court either as a palace or as a place of meeting for a judicial tribunal. Thus we speak of the Court of St. James's, or Hampton Court, as contrasted with the Court of Exchequer, or the Court of Appeal. The court of parliament embraced both those meanings, and more besides. Yet no clear line was drawn between its various functions. Characteristic of the medieval parliament was an indefinite *fusion* of functions, functions which were at once legislative, judicial, and executive. Yet they were functions which will not admit of the definitions, much less the distinctions, which we as moderns should like to attach to them. Perhaps the nearest modern parallel which can be suggested is the General Court of Massachusetts in the colonial period. Today the General Court, despite its name, is predominantly a legislative assembly; administrative, executive, and judicial functions are allocated elsewhere. But until well into the eighteenth century those functions, like those of the medieval parliament, were performed with little differentiation by one assembly. Its activities were an indefinite fusion of legislation, administration, and adjudication.

From the preceding chapter it will be plain that other matters besides what we should call strictly judicial came within the ambit of parliament's functions. In the fourteenth century questions involving finance, the administration of the kingdom, and even legislation intruded upon the earlier and primarily judicial functions.

There come before parliament questions of property in which the king is, or is supposed to be, interested: if complaints are made as to the action of the escheators or if there is a question of a man's accountability for the issues of a manor, the case is likely to be settled in parliament. Questions of franchises . . . disputes between a bishop and his chapter, disputes between native and alien merchants, grants by the king, a countess's dower, a whole miscellany of petty administrative questions are parliamentary business.[16]

For example, we learn that a coroner has been elected for Lincolnshire, and it is testified in parliament that he is a fit person.[17] Several magnates give evidence that two merchants imprisoned in the Tower are not guilty of charges against them.[18] Yet all these questions were considered ancillary to the administration of justice because no distinction between legislative, administrative, and judicial functions was perceived.

In speaking of medieval institutions, we must often be satisfied with very hazy outlines. We cannot demand the sharpness of figure which we expect when modern institutions are described. As Maitland says,

If we speak, we must speak with words; if we think, we must think with thoughts. We are moderns and our words and thoughts can not but be modern. . . . Every thought will be too sharp, every word will imply too many contrasts. We must, it is feared, use many words and qualify our every statement until we have almost contradicted it.[19]

Considerations of this sort we must constantly keep in mind while seeking to understand the institutions of a bygone

---

[16] H. G. Richardson and G. O. Sayles, *Bulletin of the Institute of Historical Research* (1931), ix. 5.
[17] *Calendar of the Close Rolls, 1339-1341*, p. 212.
[18] *Ibid.*, pp. 11-12.
[19] Maitland, *Township and Borough*, p. 22.

age. The confusion—from our standpoint, at least—which permeates the medieval attitude towards legislation and adjudication is so characteristic that we must not try to simplify it too far. Simplicity is a late product of civilization, the result of technical subtlety. It is a mistake to attribute such a characteristic to early institutional developments. "Institutions," says Professor McIlwain, "that are now narrow and definite become as we trace them back indistinguishable from others that we have always considered equally definite. To ignore this fact is fatal."[20] Today we tend to separate legislative, judicial, and administrative functions, and assign to each a separate sphere. It is then somewhat perplexing to find that "we have still to deal with legislature-made judicial sentences (such as bills of pains and penalties) and with judge-made law"[21] which do not fit the niceties of our classification.

It should not, therefore, be a source of surprise when we find that in the Middle Ages men perceived no clear distinction between the various activities of parliament. What we should call a legislative act was often couched in judicial form, as the "award" of a court. On the other hand, a judgment might take the form of an enactment, as a parliamentary statute or ordinance. And in neither case would violence be done to the habits of thought of that time. Both alike were acts of a court, done in the course of administering justice. The Statute of Bigamy, for example, which was enacted in 1276, was couched, as its name signifies, in the form of a statute;[22] but it was, nevertheless, a judicial interpretation of a papal constitution. From the middle of the thirteenth century onwards, there are abundant instances in the legal records of this fusion of functions. The replies which were given to parliamentary petitions furnish instances of what we should call a confusion between legislation and adjudication. No distinction was made throughout the Middle Ages between

---

[20] McIlwain, *The High Court of Parliament*, p. 146.
[21] T. Smith, *De Republica Anglorum* (ed. Alston), Introduction, p. xxxiv.
[22] *Statutes of the Realm*, i. 42.

the reply given to a private petition, asking for the review of a case or for some special favor, and a general petition which might result in some form of enactment. Both, again, were considered "acts" of parliament, similar and of equal form and dignity. Cases are especially numerous in the reign of Edward III. For instance, in 1366 a case arose over the interpretation of a writ. Chief Justice Thorpe declared that precedent indicated that the case should be taken into parliament, where "the Lords who made the statute stated what their intention was."[23] Here is a clear instance of parliament's interpreting a statute in litigation, a function which we should think of as primarily judicial. Similarly, the lawyers whom we meet in the later Year Books compare an act of parliament to the record of the familiar courts at Westminster.[24]

Such views were not restricted to the medieval period and were particularly prevalent in the sixteenth and early seventeenth centuries. Of the Tudor period the late A. V. Dicey wrote:

> It is impossible to draw any precise line between those offences which the Council punished, acting as a government, and those which it noticed in the character of a law court; and such a distinction, could it be made, would only mislead, for it would hide what is the characteristic feature of the period under review, the inseparable combination . . . of political and judicial authority.[25]

That attitude was equally apparent in the case of other courts, such as the Star Chamber, which exercised legislative as well as judicial powers. The same is true of the courts held by the justices of assize and justices of the peace. We learn, moreover, from the journals of the house of commons for the

---

[23] Year Books, M. 39 Ed. III, 21.

[24] S. E. Thorne, A Discourse Upon the Exposicion & Understandinge of Statutes (San Marino, 1942), p. 14. Cf. Year Books, T. 7 H. VII, 15: "Act de Parlement n'est forsque Judicium, et un Act come un Jugement."

[25] Dicey, Privy Council, p. 106. Cf. J. Hatschek, Englisches Staatsrecht (Tübingen: 1905 ff.), i. 113: "Bis zum 17 Jahrhundert war das englische Gesetz nur eine Art Urteilsspruch, judicium, und selbst heute haften noch Überreste dieser Vorstellung dem englischen Gesetzbegriffe an."

year 1589 that the Speaker quieted a commotion in the commons by reminding them that

every Member of this House is a Judge of this Court, being the highest Court of all other Courts, and the great Council also of this Realm, and so moveth them in regard thereof, that as in all other Courts . . . such confused courses either of contention, acclamations, or reciprocal bitter and sharp Speeches, terms or words are not any way either used or permitted amongst the Judges of the said Inferiour Courts.[26]

In 1595 the judges in *Chudleigh's Case* referred to the Statute of Uses (1536) as a "judgment by the whole Parliament."[27] In the seventeenth century, Sir Edward Coke explains that the king cannot require the testimony of the members of the house of commons upon things done in the house itself, because "every member of the parliament hath a judiciall place, and can be no witnesse."[28] So late, in fact, did this habit of mind persist that the first edition of Finch's *Law* contains the following statement:

The Parliament is a Court of the King, Nobility, and Commons assembled, Hauing an absolute power in all causes. As to make Lawes, to adiudge matters in Law, to trie causes of life and death; to reuerse errors in the Kings Bench, especially where any common mischiefe is, that by the ordinarie course of Law there is no meanes to remedie: this is the proper Court for it. And all Decrees are as Iudgements. And if the Parliament it selfe doe erre (as it may) it can no where be reuersed but in Parliament.[29]

The failure to differentiate between legislative and judicial functions was as characteristic of the sixteenth and seventeenth centuries as it was of the Middle Ages. Because no clear distinction was drawn, for instance, between a judgment and an enactment until the seventeenth century, people were under no compulsion to think of parliament except in terms of what it had been in the beginning, a court of justice. That

26 S. D'Ewes, *The Journals of all the Parliaments during the Reign of Queen Elizabeth* (London, 1682), p. 434.
27 1 *Coke's Reports* 132b.
28 Coke, *The Fourth Part of the Institutes of the Laws of England*, p. 15.
29 H. Finch, *Law* (London, 1627), p. 233.

people in the Middle Ages thought of parliament in this way, and of its functions as essentially judicial, is very plain. In 1311, an article in the famous Ordinances of Reform specified that parliament should be held at least once or twice a year for the redress of grievances which could not be dealt with outside of parliament.[30] Later on in the fourteenth century, as has already been shown, the commons repeatedly petitioned that parliament should be held at least once a year for the hearing of cases which had been delayed or improperly dealt with in the king's courts. Under the Tudors, in spite of the many new courts created, it became a standard grievance that justice was not done because parliaments met so infrequently. This can be seen very clearly in the preamble of the Act of 1585 concerning appeals to the Court of Exchequer Chamber:

> Forasmuch as erronious Judgementes given in the Courte called the Kinges Bench are only to be reformed by the High Courte of Parliament, which Court of Parliament is not in these Dayes so often holden as in auncient time it hath bene, neither yet in respecte of greater Affaires of this Realme such erronious Judgements can be well considered of and determined during the time of the Parliamente, whereby the Subjects of this Realme are greatly hindered and delayed of Justice in such Cases: Be it therefore enacted. . . .[31]

When the commons complained that "justice was not done" or that "cases were not heard," we are to understand that commons' petitions for the redress of general abuses of the realm were being neglected as well as private ones. They meant that they had had no opportunity to present articles on which new statutes would be based. In present-day language we should say that they were thinking fully as much of legislation as of the settlement of judicial cases. Yet the enactment of new law, based upon a petition of grievances by the commons, was not differentiated from the relief given by a judgment in consequence of the private petition of an

[30] *Statutes of the Realm*, i. 165.
[31] *Statutes of the Realm*, iv. 714.

individual. Hence enactment, like a judgment, was considered to be the decision of a court, and enactments were framed in the same manner as judgments, that is, by the judges of the court, by the king and council. Thus the position of the commons was that of petitioners only, and such their position remained throughout the Middle Ages. Changes in the law might be proposed by the commons, but it was only as the servant and petitioner of the prerogative that they could proceed. Their subordinate position in parliament, therefore, down to the seventeenth century, was in large measure a consequence of the essentially judicial character of parliament.

What gave added support to the idea of parliament as a court of justice was the persistence of the primitive idea that law was something which was already in existence, above the state, something which could be defined or promulgated by a court, but not made. In the Middle Ages it was the law which was sovereign and not the community.[32] It was not conceived that the state could alter law; law was not a matter of will but a matter of knowledge. Statutes accordingly assumed "the form of declaring existing rules or regulating the methods of procedure, and not that of deliberate innovation."[33] The frequent affirmations of existing statutes by parliaments in the fourteenth and fifteenth centuries make it plain that they regarded it as their business to assert and reassert the law. Mr. Pickthorn has pointed out that almost all the acts of the parliaments of Henry VII were "unquestionably designed for the enforcement of what no one doubted to be already law . . . by fortifying or adapting procedure, by increasing penalties, by directing police administration, by applying admitted social principles to industrial and commercial occasions."[34] As late as the time of Elizabeth, the law reports reveal that the current legal attitude towards

32 F. Kern, *Historische Zeitschrift* (1919), cxx. 11.
33 A. L. Lowell, *Essays on Government* (New York, 1889), p. 196. See also Haskins, *The Statute of York*, pp. 26-36.
34 K. Pickthorn, *Early Tudor Government* (Cambridge, 1934), i. 144-45.

statutes and enactments was that they were not innovations, but fresh definitions of already existing rules.[35] Despite the fact that considerable law was actually made by parliament in the Middle Ages, and that considerably more was made in the Tudor and Stuart periods, the early idea that statutes were affirmations of existing law persisted long after that theory no longer described the facts.[36] Such being the character of statutes, *enactment was considered the proper business of courts, whose duty it was to define and apply the law*. Because as late as the sixteenth century men thought of law as something immutable and in existence, which could be defined but not altered by the will of government, they were not driven to formulate theories about law in terms of popular sovereignty but were content to leave the power of enactment in the hands of the courts, where it had always been.

What made the judicial nature of parliament particularly conspicuous in the beginning was the fact that it was the king's court, the highest and greatest in the realm. Old ideas of the magical and sacred attributes of the kingship, combined with the power and dignity of the office, endowed the king's court with a special prominence. In the days before the courts of equity, it was the king who granted a grace and favor which could not be expected from an ordinary tribunal. Just as St. Louis had sat under the famous oak at Vincennes, so the English king opened his highest court to dispense mercy and justice to all. Here a plaintiff might bring his "bille" and hope for a justice of which the chief purpose was not the fines and the fees to be received. Parliament was the king's great and extraordinary court of justice, in which he granted redress when other courts were unable or unwilling to grant relief. In parliament

extraordinary jurisdiction was exerted on behalf of the otherwise helpless suitor; but when the process was launched, the remedy fell again into the rule, and was to be received from the ordinary tribunal. A

[35] W. S. Holdsworth, *A History of English Law* (London, 1922 ff.), iv. 183.
[36] Hatschek, *Englisches Staatsrecht*, i. 119.

prerogative above the law was exercised in consequence of the exigency of the case; but the proceeding was entirely within the compass of the law.[37]

Parliament, especially under Edward I, came to be above all the time and place for remedying private wrongs. The power of a petitioner's adversary, his own poverty, or the insufficiency of the law justified his having recourse to parliament. The fact that men brought cases from local or seignorial courts tended further to break down the power of local magnates and the sheriffs in the counties. It made possible the further consolidation of the royal administration, and it helped to develop the idea that the people were subjects of the king rather than vassals of particular lords. By making parliament into the poor man's court of first instance, and a court of appeal for cases which required skilled attention, Edward I strengthened his own position and that of parliament enormously. At the same time, as the common law began to grow, its rigidities required equitable modification. By associating that equitable relief in the public mind with himself, the king's prestige was greatly enhanced.

The large number of cases which came before parliament for settlement or review bear witness to the popularity of parliament in England. We learn that as early as 1280, the multitude of private petitions presented had become a source of much trouble. An ordinance states that "the folk who come to the king's parliament are often delayed and disturbed to the great grievance of them and of the court by the numerous petitions which are presented to the king."[38] Arrangements had therefore to be made for sorting the petitions— some to go to the Exchequer, some to the Chancery, others to the council, and still others to the king himself. Subsequently, special receivers and triers were appointed to deal with the vast numbers of petitions presented. It may fairly be said that because of the judicial relief which parliament

---

37 *Collected Historical Works of Sir Francis Palgrave,* viii. 114.
38 *Records of the Parliament of 1305,* p. lvi.

afforded, its permanent characteristic as a court of justice was by that means fostered, despite the fact that subsequently much of its remedial jurisdiction passed to the Chancellor's court of equity.

From the private petition which asked a favor or grace of the king, it was only a short step to the group petitions of general grievances such as were presented increasingly by the commons in the fourteenth century. The earliest commons' petitions are phrased in exactly the same way as private petitions. Not only is the influence of the latter clear, but the fact that the commons were thought of on the same plane as the private petitioner is especially evident. Throughout the Middle Ages, as has been said, hardly any distinction was drawn between the determination of a commons' petition, asking for the remedying of a general abuse, and a private request for judicial relief. No clear line existed between matters public and matters private. Consequently the importance of the commons in parliament arose less from the fact that they were representatives of the communities of the realm in a central assembly than from the fact that they were petitioners before the king's high court of justice. Because they, as private individuals, might petition the king for the remedy of a wrong or for an act of grace or favor, they came to present joint petitions upon their arrival in parliament. The king's need of money was one lever which they used to ensure not only the acceptance of their petitions, but the favorable answering of them. But the conception of kingly duty, which included the notion that legitimate grievances should be remedied by the king, was also a potent force in the development of the commons' power. At the same time, the procedure which the commons used tended further to exalt the king and his council. The very fact of petitioning threw into higher relief the dispensing power of the king.[39] It explains

---

[39] In 1399 it was said: "les Juggementz du Parlement appertiegnent soulement au Roy et as Seigneurs & nient as Communes." *Rotuli Parliamentorum*, iii. 427.

to a great extent the inferior position of the commons in parliament which lasted in fact and in theory until the seventeenth century.

The English parliament was not the only medieval assembly whose nature was essentially judicial, and that fact may be of some importance in accounting for the judicial aspect of parliament's activity. Several historians have been at pains to point out the differences between the parliament of England and, for example, the *parlement* of Paris.[40] What is far more striking are the similarities between the two, especially in the thirteenth century. Many records of the French *parlements* might easily be interchanged with the records of a parliament of Edward I. The redressing of wrongs through royal inquests and the settling of cases is fully as characteristic of the *parlement* of Paris as of the parliament of England. Its business, like that of other contemporary parliaments, was a mixture of the judicial, the administrative, and the political. The same is true of the thirteenth-century *Reichstag* in Germany. However, the *parlement* of Paris was not a representative assembly in the sense that the parliament of England was. The summoning of representatives of the towns in France was sporadic and was generally for purely fiscal reasons, so that they never really became involved with the full functions of the *parlement*. Besides, the French *parlement* had to perform many of the duties of the King's Bench, the Common Bench, and the justices in eyre. That fact brought its judicial work far more into the foreground in the fourteenth century.

It is accordingly worth speculating whether the judicial character of the English parliament may have owed something to ideas borrowed from France. Like problems in countries sharing a common civilization may have suggested like solutions,[41] but it seems probable also that there was a good

---

40 See W. S. Holdsworth, *Essays in Law and History* (Oxford, 1946), pp. 41-48, 51.

41 H. G. Richardson, *Transactions of the Royal Historical Society*, 4th ser. (1928), xi. 157.

deal of conscious imitation. The English king, as duke of Guyenne, was represented constantly by proctors in the *parlement*, and the personal links were extensive. There was much coming and going between *parlement* and parliament on the part of certain friars. William of Gainsborough, as Minister General of the Friars Minor, was present at a Scottish parliament of Edward I in 1292 where the question of the Scottish succession was under consideration.[42] In 1294 he is found acting as proctor for the king of England in Paris.[43] In 1297 he is at the parliament held at Westminster.[44] Later, he becomes bishop of Worcester and regularly attends the king's parliaments as a prelate. And what shall we say of the illustrious Philippe de Remi, sire de Beaumanoir, the compiler of the great treatise on law in thirteenth-century France? As an occasional poet, he sings of England and English earls and the bad French which they spoke. Was he in England and did English influence affect him? Did he know Bracton? Was he a link between the legal traditions of France and England?

We may accept the judicial nature of the English parliament as its most prominent characteristic in the fourteenth century. The admixture during that century of fiscal, political, and diplomatic business, the enlarging of the personnel, did not alter fundamentally the character of parliament in men's minds. Throughout the Middle Ages it remained the king's high court of justice. It was even argued that the taxes granted in parliament were but the revenues of that court, just as the fees taken, for example, in the court of King's Bench were the proper revenues due the crown for the administration of justice.[45] The subordinate position of the commons is very plain. Despite their increasing activities in

---

[42] W. Rishanger, *Chronica Monasterii S. Albani* (ed. Riley, Rolls Series: London, 1865), pp. 255, 260.

[43] P. Langtoft, *The Chronicle of Pierre de Langtoft* (ed. Wright, Rolls Series: London, 1866 ff.), ii. 204.

[44] *Parliamentary Writs*, i. 55.

[45] T. F. T. Plucknett, in *Tudor Studies Presented to A. F. Pollard* (London, 1924), p. 164.

the legislative sphere, their position was thought to be no different in the fifteenth century, when we find the emergence of a distinct and explicitly formulated theory as to parliament's judicial character, which helped even more to perpetuate the inferior position of the commons. The advantage of such a theory was that it "went far to explain in familiar phraseology a great deal of the outer semblance and many of the manifestations of parliamentary activity."[46] It helped to explain the relation between the king and parliament, and between parliament and the other courts of law, without having to recast old ideas about the law and the kingship. On the basis of such a theory it was not necessary "to assume or suggest that any modification had occurred in the relations of king and subject by the emergence of parliament, nor to invoke the aid of radical political ideas. Ordinary notions of royal inheritance and command, and the due process of familiar law, sufficed to explain the parliamentary phenomenon. Moreover, they were not only plausible in the face of the facts—they were also obviously true historically."[47]

Political conditions, however, and the changes which had actually taken place in parliament in the fourteenth and fifteenth centuries, meant that that theory could not long endure without modification. As early as the reign of Henry VI some lawyers had begun to perceive that "conceptions borrowed from the law as to the jurisdiction of courts could not easily be applied to those powers of taxation and legislation which were fast coming to be the most important functions of Parliament."[48] By the sixteenth century men found it possible to compare the functions of parliament to those of the council as well as to those of a court.[49] In the first place, a change had come about in the relation of the com-

46 Chrimes, *English Constitutional Ideas*, p. 77.
47 *Ibid.* Interestingly enough, the expression, "high court of parliament" begins to make its appearance on the parliament rolls at a time when its judicial functions are being superseded by its legislative functions. See Gray, *The Influence of the Commons*, p. 417.
48 Holdsworth, *Essays in Law and History*, pp. 63-64.
49 D'Ewes, *Journal*, pp. 411, 515.

mons to enactment: not merely were they the chief initiating organ for legislation, but they had successfully insisted that statute and petition should correspond textually.[50] In 1414 they had asserted that they were "as well Assentirs as Peticioners,"[51] and their claim was approved by the king. Thereafter amendments to their bills by the lords or by the king's officials were referred back to the commons and their assent obtained to the final draft of the statute. The significance of that development was that the commons thereafter were thought to share indirectly in the administration of justice, and that fact helped to combat the notion that they were only the petitioners of the crown. In the second place, parliament was observed to have extraordinary features which no mere court, however high, could possess. It had a unique capacity for binding all by its "judgments"—a capacity which no ordinary court of law could be supposed to have.[52] In 1376 Chief Justice Thorpe stated that "as soon as parliament has decided anything, the law holds that everyone has knowledge of it, for parliament represents the body of all the realm."[53] Other judges and lawyers made similar observations in the fifteenth century.[54] When we find that people were prepared to think of parliament as a representative assembly rather than as exclusively a court, it became possible for them to think of its acts as binding more because they were made or approved by the nation's representatives than because they had the sanction of judgments given by the king's highest court. Such an idea could not gain headway, however, while feudal doctrine continued to be the only doctrine upon public matters. In the third place, it was an undoubted fact that by the end of the fifteenth century the great bulk of parliament's activity had come to be the framing and enacting of statutes

[50] *Rotuli Parliamentorum*, iv. 22.
[51] *Ibid.*
[52] An act of parliament did not in the fourteenth century bind the ancient demesne of the crown, but that limitation began to disappear in the late fifteenth century. See Thorne, *A Discourse Upon the Statutes*, pp. 15 ff., 31-32.
[53] Quoted by Chrimes, *English Constitutional Ideas*, p. 76.
[54] *Year Books*, T. 3 Ed. IV, 2, pl. 1; M. 21 Ed. IV, 45, pl. 6; H. 21 H. VII. 1, pl. 1.

—business which we today would call legislative. Moreover, Chancery and the council had long been encroaching on the judicial sphere of parliament, and many cases which would formerly have been the business of parliament had come to be the province of those tribunals. Other judicial business it was found convenient to have handled by small bodies, such as the Star Chamber, where only the judges and certain officials would be present.

Those changes in the function and position of parliament were nevertheless scarcely perceived by most men in the sixteenth century.[55] To them parliament was still a court and not a legislature which could alter the law by its mere will. That fact helped to account for the subordinate position of the commons in parliament until the seventeenth century. "It required time, a long time, and great changes in the state . . . to alter all this and subordinate the old idea of a court to the newer one of a legislature."[56] It required the decline of class feeling, a broader distribution of wealth and culture, a wider political self-consciousness, along with sharp ecclesiastical and civil controversies, to teach men that the high court of parliament had become the sovereign legislature of the kingdom.

Parliament, during the course of its history, has had associated with it two significant characteristics. One is its judicial character; the other is its representative character. The significance of the latter has enormously increased, whereas that of the former has almost disappeared. Yet both have been persistent facts for long periods of time, and neither can be overlooked. The persistence until the seventeenth century of the idea that parliament was essentially the king's highest court of justice was one of the most important formative influences on the growth of popular government.

55 McIlwain, *The High Court of Parliament*, pp. 121-131.
56 *Ibid.*, p. 120.

THE LATER MIDDLE AGES:
PREJUDICE AND PROMISE

THE real problem in the history of parliament, it has been rightly said, is not so much to explain the beginnings of certain modern practices in the house of commons as to attempt to show why popular representation became an essential and inseparable feature of parliament.[1] Parliament began as the king's own court, and it has become a representative assembly. Marked as the changes have been in the structure and complexion of parliament, the use of elected representatives has been a persistent feature of parliament since the thirteenth century. In the course of time that feature has become a dominant and basic fact in modern political institutions.

The problem is not to be clarified by any search into origins, no matter how ingenious or far-reaching. The house of commons, as we know it today, may be said to date mainly from the seventeenth century; most of its procedure from the eighteenth and nineteenth centuries. The explanation is therefore to be found in tracing the increasing activities of the modern period; it is to be found in tracing the new ideas consequent upon these activities, which resulted in the commons coming to be considered as an essential part of the machinery of parliament. It was the grafting of new ideas and practices onto the old institution which brought about the transformation of the medieval into the modern parliament.

Parliament began in the thirteenth century as an expanded session of the king's council. Administrative expedience and financial needs had caused the king to summon before his

[1] H. G. Richardson, *Transactions of the Royal Historical Society*, 4th ser. (1928), xi. 170.

council at Westminster not only the magnates and greater barons, but elected representatives of the counties and towns. But these representatives appeared only by royal command, and they treated upon those matters in which the king was interested. Throughout the fourteenth and the greater part of the fifteenth centuries, parliament was in a very real sense the king's court. The magnates and representatives in the fourteenth century were scarcely more than the servants and petitioners of the prerogative, and their wishes and grievances were redressed only insofar as they were accepted by the king and council. Compared with the great legislating parliaments of later days, the role of the commons was a passive one.

By the sixteenth century, however, parliament had emerged as a representative assembly of three estates, consisting, in the words of Sir Edward Coke, "of the kings majesty sitting there as in his royall politick capacity, and of the three estates of the realm: viz. of the lords spiritual . . . the lords temporall . . . and the commons."[2] In the mid-seventeenth century there emerged a distinct conception of parliament as a legislative assembly, whose powers were wielded largely by the house of commons, rather than by the king and council as in a high court of justice. The steps by which this transformation from the medieval to the modern parliament took place were slow and microscopic, but the contrast between parliament in 1350 and 1650 is nevertheless striking. How did this transformation come about?

To the historians of an elder generation, to men like Gneist and Hallam and Stubbs, parliament had been consciously founded by Edward I upon a system of estates perfected in 1295. Such doctrines at times infected even Maitland, who stated that "before the end of the thirteenth century the national assembly is ceasing to be a feudal court; it is becom-

2 Coke, *Fourth Institute*, c. 1.

ing an assembly of the estates of the realm."[3] Recent investigation of the activities of parliament, and particularly of the representatives, indicates that this description is not accurate. It was not until well on in the fourteenth century that the commons acquired control over finance and secured much power of initiative in enactment. Even then, the stage had not been reached when the commons' petitions were converted automatically by engrossment into statutes. The enacting power belonged exclusively to the king's judges and the members of the council. So late as 1389, it was necessary for the commons to petition that the chancellor and council should make no ordinances conflicting with the common law after a session of parliament had been dismissed.[4]

In the fourteenth century parliament was above all a court to secure redress for exceptional hardships of individuals and of the people at large. This fact further emphasized the inferior position of the commons in parliament; it helped to confine their activities. Their position was that of suitors at a court; whether one looks at their financial or legislative functions, this is apparent. Even the grants which they made the king were considered to be no more than the revenues of the king's high court. In a striking speech in court in 1441, Chief Baron Fray remarked: "If there were no law there would be no King and no inheritance. Now, by this law he is to have all the amercements and revenues of his courts."[5] In other words, parliamentary taxation was thought to be a profit of the king's court of parliament to which he was entitled in the same way as to the fines of the King's Bench.

So distinct were these ideas about parliament and the position of the commons, so marked the expositions of it, that it is impossible to accept the position of historians like Stubbs and Hallam. Their notion that by 1400 the structure of the

---

[3] F. W. Maitland, *The Constitutional History of England* (Cambridge, 1908), p. 75.
[4] *Rotuli Parliamentorum*, iii. 266.
[5] Quoted by T. F. T. Plucknett, in *Tudor Studies Presented to A. F. Pollard*, p. 164.

English government was complete and that the fifteenth century was "startlingly and prematurely modern," a period of
"unbroken constitutional government," scarcely describes the
facts of the situation. These historians, in their enthusiasm
for representative institutions, believed that the knights and
burgesses in the fifteenth century were on the whole an up-
standing and honorable class of people. The fact that greater
advances in parliamentary government were not made in the
century they attributed to the wickedness of the times and to
the absence of public spirit among the great lords. "If the
only object of Constitutional History," says Stubbs, "were
the investigation of the origin and powers of Parliament, the
study of the subject might be suspended at the deposition of
Richard II."[6] In his sanguine view, not only was the structure
of parliament complete in 1400, but "never before and never
again for more than two hundred years were the commons
so strong as they were under Henry IV."[7]

It is pointless to seize upon every increase in the power of
the commons in this period and to hold it up as a victory for
popular government. As Mr. Jolliffe says, "To do so is to
read into the second century of parliamentary history the
common will and purpose, the reasoned jealousy for its rights
and powers, the fuller sense of its place in the constitution,
which only came to parliament after it had fought its way
to predominance against the Stuarts."[8] It is equally purpose-
less to preach moral sermons on the decadence of an age
which does not exemplify issues or principles which another
generation considers significant. The protracted wars, the
many private feuds which fill the pages of the annals of the
fifteenth century, are symptomatic of a general breakdown in
the structure of medieval society. It is an age of uncertainty,
of many conflicting ideas and sentiments; it is characterized
by a general lack of fundamental convictions on every side.

6 Stubbs, *Constitutional History*, iii. 2.
7 *Ibid.*, p. 73.
8 Jolliffe, *Constitutional History*, p. 441.

Yet these matters are to be considered objectively for the light they throw upon the subject of our investigation.

In the fifteenth century, the breakdown of the medieval community is everywhere apparent. "The central judicature was losing its independence. . . . Judgments, when rightly rendered, were made valueless by falsification, perversions of the verdicts really returned, or erasure from the rolls, and in the provincial courts it was often impossible to obtain any sort of record by which a case might be carried in appeal."[9] Private wars were carried on on a wide scale. In 1417, we learn from a parliamentary petition that large bands of associated malefactors were ravaging the country, plundering the people, holding the forests, spreading Lollardy, treason, and rebellion.[10] Several counties were infested with bandits, and the scholars of Oxford were waging a war of their own against the county.[11] Legal severities, even torture, had no effect on reducing the general anarchy.

The old nobility was fast disappearing, and a new chivalry was growing up which cut across the old feudal ties. Their power was fostered by maintenance and livery. The small man took a lord's livery, and the guilt of the great went unquestioned. Corruption permeated society. The records show that assize jurors were constantly bought, and that the sheriffs were the tools of great men. One gets the impression of general disillusionment in an age when old beliefs had gone and new ones had not yet come in to take their place. The spread of Lollardy among the poorer classes is simply another symptom of dissatisfaction with the older order. There is much talk of the dignity of the individual, as against the artificial rule of law. One feels that "the dead-weight of indifference and disillusionment paralysed those who had the task of maintaining law and order upon the established principles."[12]

The "aggressive policy," the "rare initiative" which Stubbs

9 *Ibid.*, p. 414.
10 *Rotuli Parliamentorum*, iv. 113; cf. *ibid.*, iv. 24.
11 Stubbs, *Constitutional History*, iii. 278.
12 Jolliffe, *Constitutional History*, p. 422.

speaks of as characteristic of the house of commons in the fifteenth century would indeed be a marvelous thing in the midst of the general breakdown in society—that is, it would be, if it were true. Close scrutiny of the records shows that the parliaments of Lancaster and York were often ancillary to the council and shared in the general characteristics of the government of that time. The political and dynastic crises from 1388 on dragged parliament more or less unwillingly in their train, but dragged them none the less. The commons were used to give the color of wide popular support and to give the sanction of law to victories gained by factions. Such strength as the commons had in the reign of Henry IV was not theirs but their lords', who, however divided, were at least stronger than the king. "Almost without exception, parliament appears as the tool rather than the maker of revolutions. The Merciless Parliament of 1388 met under the influence of the Appellants. It sat under the menace of the armed companies of Gloucester, Warwick, and Arundel."[13] Much of the appearance of spontaneity in the commons' actions was the consequence of intimidation and packing. In 1455 the Duchess of Norfolk wrote to John Paston, saying, "It is thought right necessarie . . . that my Lord have at this tyme in the Parlement suche persones as longe unto him, and be of his menyall servaunts."[14] Another letter of the same year in the Paston collection recites that, "Sum men holde it right straunge to be in this Parlement, and me thenketh they be wyse men that soo doo."[15]

How common such packing was, of course, we cannot be sure, for it is not entirely safe to generalize from the isolated instances which we know of.[16] The influence of the magnates upon the knights was to a certain extent inevitable. It could

13 Ibid., p. 443.
14 The Paston Letters (ed. Gairdner: London, 1872), no. 244.
15 Ibid., no. 249.
16 On this question, see H. G. Richardson, "John of Gaunt and the Parliamentary Representation of Lancashire," Bulletin of the John Rylands Library (1938), xxii. 175.

scarcely be otherwise when the knights were their tenants, their servants, their comrades in arms. But it must be remembered that the knights were for the most part self-respecting country gentlemen, men who had had considerable experience in administrative affairs in one way or another. Many of them were no doubt offended at the idea of allowing themselves to be merely the tools of faction. Many more must have been concerned not to commit themselves and, above all, not to make themselves conspicuous in the quarrels of the mighty.

The generally unsettled character of the fifteenth century had a distinct influence upon the election to parliament of the knights and burgesses. As a force in local affairs, the county court had suffered in the previous hundred years a marked decline. No longer was every freeholder expected to attend personally the monthly sessions of the court. Many of its functions had been turned over to the justices of the peace, while most of its judicial work now concerned pleas of debt. Consequently the only persons whose attendance was required personally were the parties to suits and the rota of qualified jurors. Since no others were required, and since parliamentary elections were still held in full county court, it is easy to see that the electors were not representative of the county and might be persons of little substance, people who might easily be intimidated by the sheriff. A statute in 1406 enacted that for the occasion of an election, other persons than the normal suitors were to be specially cited. Provision was also made to see that the power of the sheriffs to cite electors was not abused.[17] Yet in spite of these provisions it is clear that elections were often carried through in the absence of the better people of the county, or were dispatched by the rabble.[18] Such too was the power of the sheriffs that precautions had to be taken against their falsifying returns, and an elaborate system of indentures, signed or sealed by the suitors,

[17] *Statutes of the Realm*, ii. 156.
[18] *Rotuli Parliamentorum*, ii. 355. Cf. *Statutes of the Realm*, ii. 243.

were required to be sent in by the sheriff with his return. A fine of £100 was exacted from any sheriff who was discovered to have manipulated the returns.[19]

Knights and burgesses in the fifteenth century appear on occasion anxious to be elected to parliament. However, we cannot be too sure that it was high-minded motives and public spirit which induced men to stand for parliament, as Stubbs alleges. It must first be asked whether there were not ulterior motives in seeking election. Clearly some knights had other business in view at Westminster, possibly even their pleasure. We know for certain that many lawyers who sought election in parliament had in mind combining litigation before the courts with their duties as knights of the shire.[20] Some borough representatives, required for other purposes, considered election as a way of defraying the expenses of a journey to London.[21]

Promise there was, however, among the conflicting and discouraging tendencies of the fifteenth century. Attempts were constantly made to secure the return of suitable men of ability to parliament. An act of 1382 forbade the sheriff to omit the regular cities or boroughs from his returns and thus tamper with the elections.[22] Apparently he had been using his influence to distinguish the right of certain boroughs to return representatives. In 1404, a petition from Rutland indicates that the sheriff at times was able to return members who had not been duly elected.[23] Other acts in the fifteenth century attempted to regulate elections and to insist on certain qualifications for representatives. Constantly the king tried to secure real knights "girt with a sword" and "more approved by feats of arms." In 1445 he asserted that the persons chosen for parliament should be notable knights of the

---

19 *Statutes of the Realm*, ii. 341.
20 Stubbs, *Constitutional History*, iii. 421.
21 Cf. K. Wood-Legh, *English Historical Review* (1931), xlvi. 374-75.
22 *Statutes of the Realm*, ii. 25.
23 *Rotuli Parliamentorum*, iii. 530.

shire which elected them, or else notable squires, gentlemen of birth capable of becoming knights, and that "no man of the degree of yeoman or below it shall be eligible."[24]

Other statutes specified qualifications for the electors. In 1430, in the eighth year of Henry VI, a restrictive act was passed which remained in force until the nineteenth century. Whereas, it runs, by great attendance of "People of small Substance and no Value, whereof every of them pretended a Voice equivalent, as to such Elections to be made, with the most worthy Knights and Esquires,"[25] improper persons are returned to parliament, it is enacted that only resident persons possessed of a freehold worth forty shillings a year or more should be allowed to vote. Two years later, it was ordered that the qualifying freehold should be within the county.[26]

There are signs, too, towards the end of the century, that parliamentary election was regarded by some as less of a burden and more as a way to preferment at home or at the court. When we find men at pains to dispute an election,[27] when we find men standing for parliament in more than one constituency, when we find men in parliament who have been in many other parliaments, we may then say that people in the street have become interested in the affairs of the kingdom. Their first interest has ceased to be in resisting taxation. Newsletters are circulated,[28] the people of the counties and towns demand a full report of the affairs of parliament from their representatives when they return, and a view wider than the constituency is in process of formation, a view which will find its eloquent expression in the eighteenth century in Burke's famous speech to his constituents in Bristol.

The size of the commons in the fifteenth century was about

[24] Lords' Report on the Dignity of a Peer, iv. 913, 920, 924, etc.; Statutes of the Realm, ii. 340-42.
[25] Statutes of the Realm, ii. 243.
[26] Ibid., ii. 273.
[27] Cf. Stubbs, Constitutional History, iii. 438.
[28] For an early newsletter, see H. G. Richardson and G. O. Sayles, English Historical Review (1938), liii. 436-37.

half what it is today. Generally about three hundred persons appeared in answer to the summons. The returns indicate that there were generally something over two hundred burgesses, and about seventy-four knights of the shire. We find that the commons frequently forget that their summons once depended upon the pleasure of the king. In 1377 they assert, "By common right of the realm there are and ought to be two persons elected from every county in England to be in Parliament for the commune of the said counties."[29] They also claim favorable points of procedure as the "ancient custom and form of Parliament."[30]

In parliament, the commons debated on most matters of public interest. Foreign policy, diplomacy, and the general affairs of the kingdom were discussed. For example, in 1446 the Treaty of Troyes was made with their consent. In 1427 they petitioned the king to intercede with the pope on behalf of Archbishop Chichele, who was threatened by Martin V with suspension from his legation. Their freedom of debate had been assured them by Henry IV, and their right to criticize the king's ministers had been asserted in the impeachments of Latimer and Pole. In 1406 they had asked permission to audit accounts, and Henry had replied that kings do not render accounts.[31] But in the next year the accounts were laid before the commons without their asking for them, and the victory so secured was never again formally challenged. The privilege of freedom from arrest for themselves and their retainers during a parliamentary session was secured by the commons early in the fifteenth century. In spite of the famous case of Speaker Thorpe in 1453, the privilege was seldom disregarded.

As the agency through which most petitions of a general nature were presented to the crown, the commons grew to still further importance in the first half of the fifteenth cen-

29 *Rotuli Parliamentorum,* ii. 368.
30 *Ibid.*
31 Stubbs, *Constitutional History,* iii. 55.

tury. The magnates under Richard II had fused more and more with the council and had shed their function of corporate petitioning. They now acted as the crown's agents for transmitting the commons' requests. It is plain that a committee of magnates was appointed by the king to deal with commons' petitions, and that the lords themselves frequently had their requests framed along with the commons' in the general petition. This operated to exalt the commons' petitions as the normal method of bringing about changes in the law or of securing the redress of grievances.[32]

Modern as the house of commons may appear in the fifteenth century, the development was premature and a good deal of the impression is illusory. Many of the advances achieved by the commons under the Lancastrians were lost or eclipsed under the Yorkists and early Tudors. Under Edward IV, parliaments were held increasingly less than before. In his reign of twenty-two years he held but six. Henry VII between 1485 and 1509 held only seven. In the second half of the fifteenth century, many important commons' bills were rejected, and the crown became increasingly active in legislation at the expense of the commons. Crown bills, based on no previous petition by lords or commons, became increasingly common, and there was little pretense made at popular initiative.

This decline in the power and importance of the commons led Stubbs to say that the period of the Lancastrians was one of unbroken constitutional government, whereas that of the Yorkists was characterized by a complete disregard of moral principles and constitutional restraints. That description is not sufficiently objective; it is too facile, too superficial to be accepted. The real explanation of the prominence or obscurity of the commons seems to have depended on the actual power of the crown. When the crown was strong, the magnates and the commons were weak. When the crown was weak,

---

[32] On the relation between law and public opinion in medieval England, see the thoughtful paper of H. M. Cam, *The Legislators of Medieval England* (British Academy: London, 1946).

parliament might gain in authority, but it could never hold it, for the resources of government were still medieval. The commons in the fifteenth century were either petitioners or critics. Reflecting generally the political color of the moment, they never shared with the king and lords the responsibilities of government as equal participators.

Other factors explain somewhat the decline of parliament under the Yorkists. One was the rivalry between the council and parliament over jurisdiction; another was the growth of new courts which handled many cases and which even supplemented the legislation of parliament. The crown exercised judicial and legislative power through the Court of Star Chamber, for example. Though primarily a judicial tribunal, this court "participated in the legislative powers usurped by the King and his Council. The Star Chamber not only expounded the laws, but even made laws."[33] Cases in equity were now handled largely by the Court of Chancery, so that fewer petitions of grace and favor came before parliament. Finally, the cost of litigation in parliament had grown excessively and operated to diminish the need for such long sessions. A memorandum, the only one of its kind, survives from the fifteenth century to show us the "costage and expens for to sywe to the Kyng and the counseyll." Among the items were charges for making three successive bills; there were several letters of the privy seal and copies to be paid for; there were an equal number of fees to the king's secretary; a fee "to a squyer of my lord pryvy seall for to help yt yit mygth de seled"; fees to the secretary of the chamberlain and to the chancellor's registrar; "wyne to squyers and other genthilmen at dyverse tymys"; a fish for the lord chancellor, and lampreys for some one else; to say nothing of sums "for rydying and costage to London and for his labour & his horse."[34]

33 C. L. Scofield, *The Court of Star Chamber* (Chicago, 1900), p. 49.
34 Baldwin, *The King's Council*, pp. 533-34. Later examples may be found in *Select Cases in the Star Chamber* (ed. Leadam, Selden Society: London, 1911), ii. 196 ff.

In spite of the fact that the number of sessions of parliament declined, and the activities of the commons diminished, the habits of action acquired over two hundred years were not to be lost in a generation or two. On the other hand, the constitutional aspect of the first half of the fifteenth century, together with the prominence of the commons, has been exaggerated by those historians who morally approve of the Lancastrian kings. At the same time, the decline under the Yorkists has been overstressed. If there had not been some advance in both practice and ideas in the fifteenth century, we should not find at the end of the century certain distinctly modern views of parliament as an assembly of three estates. The century did not see the beginning of the modern house of commons; that was the work of the civil wars of the seventeenth century. But it did bridge the gap between the two views of parliament—the older one of parliament as the king's high court of justice, the other and newer one as an assembly representing the communities of the realm, a joint enterprise in which the king, lords, and commons were spoken of together.

This clear dichotomy of ideas was the outcome on the one hand of the original nature of parliament as the *curia regis,* and on the other of the representative character of parliament as an assembly of elected men who came with full powers to bind their constituencies. The gap was bridged in part by the necessity of acknowledging the increased share of the commons in parliamentary business. In enactment, finance, and diplomacy their share had become explicit, even if the king retained the power of ultimate decision. In other ways the importance of the commons had been acknowledged. It was partly by their sanction that both the deposition of Richard II and the accession of Henry IV were carried through. "It became more and more common, as the century passed, to regard parliament—both in official and in popular contexts—as composed of the three estates of the realm, and therefore as an assembly possessing an authority innate in the natural social orders as well as an authority inherent in the king's court."[35]

The views of a man like Bishop Russell, who was chancellor in 1483, are of importance in showing the political and constitutional ideas which were current in his day. His drafted speeches are of great significance. In a speech prepared to be delivered in the parliament of Edward V (which, of course, never met) he wrote:

> The policie in christian Remes schewethe over alle yn the dayes that we be yn, how theyr public body is compowned of iij notable partes, of the prince, the nobles, and the peuple. And ther fore havynge to speke at thys tyme of alle iij as they be nowe here assembled for the wele of thys most nobylle and famous Reme of Englond, I have taken a trimembrid text suche as I fowned yn the divine servise of yestirdayes fest, the whyche to my purpose implyethe the present astate of owre nobles, owre commons, and of owre glorious prince and kynge Edward the Vth here present.[36]

Predominant, however, in the fourteenth and fifteenth centuries, was the notion of parliament as a court. It was an idea which did not completely disappear until well on in the seventeenth century. But the important thing is that alongside with it grew up a set of notions which conceived parliament as a representative assembly, quite apart from any attributes it might have as a court. Characteristically judicial as the functions of parliament might be, it was "impossible to describe the entire parliamentary phenomenon solely in terms of a court, however high and mighty."[37] As early as 1376, Chief Justice Thorpe had stated:

> Though proclamation has not been made in the county, everyone is held to know a statute from the time it was made in parliament, for as

[35] Chrimes, *English Constitutional Ideas*, p. 140.
[36] *Ibid.*, p. 123.
[37] *Ibid.*, p. 76. On this point, see the paper of J. G. Edwards, "The *Plena Potestas* of the English Parliamentary Representatives" in *Oxford Essays Presented to H. E. Salter*. Mr. Edwards suggests that the legal sovereignty of parliament had a double root: the character of parliament as a high court, and the "full powers" of the representatives of the commons. In other words, the fusion of ideas which takes place in the fifteenth century is implicit in the nature of parliament in the thirteenth.

soon as parliament has decided anything, the law holds that everyone
has knowledge of it, for parliament represents the body of all the realm,
and therefore proclamation is not necessary unless the statute itself
requires it.[38]

This notion of parliament as a representative assembly
occurs at intervals in the fifteenth century, especially in the
reigns of Henry V and Edward IV. The idea of everyone's
being party and privy to parliament particularly helped to
carry forward that "notion of parliament as a representative
assembly which was destined to qualify very substantially any
theory of it as merely one among other courts."[39] For it was
only a step from this "to the idea of an act of parliament as
deriving its force less from the fact that it had the sanction of
the king in his court and more from the fact that every man
in England was party and therefore privy to it."[40]

The assimilation of these divergent ideas had to take place
before there could be any suggestion that parliament possessed an authority distinguishable from the authority of a
high court. By the end of the fifteenth century the dichotomy
had been to a great extent bridged, and the authority of
parliament was thus "a compound of the king's own assent
with the assent of at least a majority of the lords spiritual and
temporal, and of at least a majority of the members of the
house of commons," representing the whole community of
the realm.[41] "Upon the votes of such an assembly as this the
sovereign lord king depended for his law-making and tax-
levying. By the advice and assent of his lords spiritual and
temporal and his commons in parliament assembled, and by
the authority of the same, he ordained, established, and
enacted."[42]

This new view of parliament as an assembly of estates
coöperating with the king took definite shape under the

[38] Quoted by Chrimes, *English Constitutional Ideas*, p. 76.
[39] *Ibid.*, p. 79.
[40] *Ibid.*, pp. 79-80.
[41] *Ibid.*, p. 141.
[42] *Ibid.*

Tudors. It is stated with exceptional clarity in a famous speech made by Henry VIII to the commons. "We be informed by our judges," he said, "that at no time do we stand so highly in our estate royal as in the time of parliament, wherein we as head and you as members are conjoined and knit together in one body politic."[43]

For the commons, the significant development was, as Mr. Chrimes says, "their grasp of the notion that they were come to parliament to represent not merely a number of local communities, but an estate: the commons of all the realm."[44] This view, together with the unity they achieved in parliament as a separate house, fortified the position of the commons. "They render," wrote Barbaro of the members of parliament in 1551, "the absolute and royal power legitimate."[45] But the house of commons became under the Tudors more than a formality of government; it became the recognized voice of public opinion, "more audible than ever before, a voice which Tudors might not always welcome but which they never wholly failed to heed."[46] The commons could now and then become vociferous, especially when money was asked. "Westminster was not far removed in place or feeling from the streets round St. Paul's where there were great merchants, more assertive than ever, and more listened to."[47] Opposition was often prolonged, and one of Thomas Cromwell's cherished bills was four years in passing the house.[48]

In the sixteenth century, however, participation and coöperation, what the Germans call *Mitregierungsrecht,* was far more characteristic of the commons than any consistent attempt at opposition legislation. The king and council were

43 Above, Chapter I, note 3.
44 Chrimes, *English Constitutional Ideas,* p. 141.
45 Quoted by W. Notestein, *Proceedings of the British Academy* (1924-1925), xi. 126.
46 *Ibid.*
47 *Ibid.,* p. 129.
48 R. B. Merriman, *Life and Letters of Thomas Cromwell* (Oxford, 1902), i. 123.

still supreme, for no notion of legislative sovereignty had yet made its appearance. Most bills were introduced to the commons by a committee of the privy council, and crown officials frequently nursed them along at one stage or another. Although provision was made for members to introduce bills of their own, they seldom made great use of the opportunities offered. Certainly few acts were passed without the sanction of the privy council. The program of a session was planned in advance by the crown. The crown was interested in results, and generally got them.

By the end of Elizabeth's reign, however, things were changing. The membership of the commons began to respond to the great economic advances, at home and on the sea, which had characterized the Elizabethan Age. The members returned by the boroughs were more prominent persons, men with a policy in view, who were less moved by the opinions and sentiments of the lords and other great men. The introduction of a committee system for dealing with bills began to filch from Cecil and his colleagues much of the work of drawing up measures. The up-country members realized their increased chances of successfully putting forward private bills, and they did not hesitate to do so. The house, therefore, began to respond more sensitively to what the country at large was thinking.

Impetus was given to these new tendencies at the accession of James I. James did not understand England or the Tudor government. His point of view was foreign. He failed, for one thing, to secure the election to the commons of influential privy councilors, men who would guide bills through the committee stages. He made no attempt to control elections and secure a favorable majority in the house. More than that he antagonized the commons with too many messages and with too much talk, too much theorizing about the "divine right" by which he ruled. Opposition began, tentative at first, but more pronounced as the seventeenth century advanced. In 1604, in the famous Commons' Apology, it was stated:

With all humble and due respect to Your Majesty . . . our privileges and liberties are our right and due inheritance, no less than our very lands and goods. . . . They cannot be withheld from us, denied or impaired, but with apparent wrong to the whole state of the realm.[49]

The steps by which the opposition of the commons was slowly crystallized, and by which the house began to take a firm stand against the king, need not be traced. It has been admirably recounted by Professor Notestein in his brilliant essay, "The Winning of the Initiative by the House of Commons." By the 1620's the commons had not only attained a great degree of political self-consciousness, a self-consciousness which had been fostered by the new individualism and the new religious feelings born of the Reformation, but they had actually seized the reins in parliament. A change in personnel had brought to the fore men who were less subservient to the royal and conciliar will. "Lawyers crowded into the Commons and brought with them not only legal skill but initiative. Along with lawyers came antiquarians, who searched out precedents to give sanction to the new leadership."[50] Precedents from the age of Edward III and Henry IV were uncovered in the Tower and in the private accumulations of manuscripts, such as that of Sir Robert Cotton—precedents which seemed to men of the seventeenth century proof of the privileges, rights, and power of the commons at an early date. To them, "old wars, old peace, old arts that cease" were as yesterday. "Long before Stubbs and Gneist had used the printed rolls of Parliament, Cotton, Noy, and Hakewill read the rolls in manuscript and out of them forged chains to bind fast Stuart kings."[51]

By the third decade of the seventeenth century, the commons were in charge of the initiation, formulation, and pas-

49 G. W. Prothero, *Select Statutes* (Oxford, 1913), p. 288.
50 W. Notestein, *Proceedings of the British Academy* (1924-25), xi. 169.
51 *Ibid.*, xi. 173.

sage of laws. They were the tail that wagged the dog. John Selden could remark, "The house of Comons is called ye Lower house in Twenty Acts of Parliam^t. But what are Twenty Acts of parliament (amongst ffrends)?"[52] By the 1640's, the wheel had come full circle. In the Militia Act of 1642, the commons repudiated for the first time the fiction of parliament as a court and transferred to themselves the sovereign authority attributed to the king "by lawyers in his ideal character. They assumed to themselves the supreme power of the state, retaining nothing of monarchy but the name."[53]

It was asserted in the Militia Act:

> It is acknowledged that the King is the Fountain of Justice and Protection, but the Acts of Justice and Protection are not exercised in his own Person, nor depend upon his pleasure but by his Courts. . . . The High Court of Parliament is not only a Court of Judicature, enabled by the Laws to adjudge and determine the Rights and Liberties of the Kingdom . . . but it is likewise a Council to provide for the necessity, to prevent the imminent Dangers, and preserve the publick Peace and Safety of the Kingdom.[54]

"By this memorable declaration," says John Allen, "which was the groundwork of all the subsequent proceedings of the parliament in the civil wars that ensued, it is obvious that the two houses . . . separated the politic from the natural capacity of the King."[55]

The modern house of commons was born.

If the story of the evolution of parliament is important, it is not because of its antiquity or its curiously varied history. More significant than the variations in the institutional framework is the persistence of certain permanent characteristics of the institution. In the course of the seven centuries

---

52 *Table Talk of John Selden* (ed. Pollock: London, 1927), p. 33.
53 J. Allen, *Inquiry into the Rise and Growth of the Royal Prerogative in England* (London, 1849), pp. 83-84.
54 J. Rushworth, *Historical Collections* (London, 1692), iv. 551-52.
55 Allen, *Growth of the Royal Prerogative*, p. 83.

of its history, parliament has been the tool of monarchs, oligarchs, and democratists; yet the presence of elected representatives has been constant since the thirteenth century. Today, representative institutions are a basic fact in government; and it is to be observed that in politics, as in medicine or law, the most constant phenomena are on the whole the most important.

The history of parliament has an added importance in illustrating significant uniformities in the actions and behavior of men. Because of the persistence of representation as a characteristic of modern institutions, people's sentiments have in the course of time become inextricably attached both to parliament and to representative institutions. Myths have been developed to perpetuate them, and fictions have been elaborated to explain changes in terms of the old and the familiar; with the result that parliamentary government in England today is little short of a jumble of shams which have been unconsciously worked out to justify the changes which have actually occurred.

Too often, however, there is a tendency to ignore the commonplace, to take an institution for granted because it exists; or else to seek to justify it with complicated rationalizations. Too often, also, when the institution is studied, it is studied as such, rather than as an artifice which contributes to the stability of the social equilibrium. Institutions are really no more than the symbols, the rationalizations of the sentiments of society. They are abstractions, chiefly constructed on observed uniformities in concrete acts.[56] Institutions must be studied as such, as part of the "folklore" of an age, rather than as fundamental or immutable principles.

Until recently, the objectiveness of historians who described the beginnings of parliamentary institutions was not very marked. Bishop Stubbs and E. A. Freeman, for example, were forever intent on searching for early instances of the unity and the power of the commons in the thirteenth century, or

---

[56] See Barnard, *The Functions of the Executive*, p. 286.

for evidence of the resuscitation of the primitive Germanic freedom which they thought had been chained in by autocratic kings.[57] To some extent this point of view was the result of the writings of the antiquarians of the Elizabethan and Stuart ages, men like Cotton, Coke, D'Ewes, and Prynne, who, for purposes of propaganda, conjured into medieval history "a golden age of parliamentary liberties." Because they attempted to justify the authority of the seventeenth century house of commons with precedents drawn indiscriminately from the age of Edward III, "history was set in bondage to a myth, the influence of which has not easily spent itself."[58] Stubbs's point of view was further reinforced by wishful thinking common to Victorian liberals, who believed implicitly in progress and in the sacredness of democracy as they saw it in the nineteenth-century house of commons. They set for half a century historical standards by which the evolution of the house of commons was to be described.

But as the haze cast by seventeenth-century constitutionalism and nineteenth-century democracy begins to clear, certain features of the beginnings of representative government are distinctly revealed. In the first place, it is clear that the house of commons did not grow up in response to any urge to self-government inherent in the Anglo-Saxon blood. Nor was there any act of creation on the part of Simon de Montfort or Edward I, prompted by sentiments of liberty or democracy. Parliaments were called in the beginning because they facilitated the collection of aids and enabled the king more easily to centralize his administration. The steps by which representatives came to be called regularly to meet before the council were taken to meet certain immediate

[57] Such views were not restricted to the nineteenth century. See the statement of Giovanni Michiel, quoted *Calendar of State Papers, Venetian, 1556-1557*, p. 1052: "It is certain that at the beginning, when the Parliaments were ordained, and for many subsequent years, their licence and security were so great that the most insignificant members seated in them might without any danger (even had he spoken against the King's person) have said freely whatever he thought most becoming patriotic zeal and the common weal."

[58] J. E. Neale, in *Tudor Studies Presented to A. F. Pollard*, p. 257.

needs, without a thought of possible ultimate consequences. The lack of direction toward the ultimate end arrived at is one of the most prominent facts in the evolution of the house of commons.

Parliament remained throughout the Middle Ages essentially what it had been in the thirteenth century—a strongly reinforced session of the king's council. Essentially parliament was a court, devised to dispense a kind of higher justice; its business appeared, until the seventeenth century, as largely judicial. Even what we should call its "legislative" acts were regarded merely as the decisions of new cases. This characteristic of parliament affected fundamentally the position of the representative element. In spite of their increasing activities in finance, legislation, and administration, the commons remained through at least the sixteenth century the servant and petitioner of the prerogative in the king's high court of parliament. Their ultimate consolidation too was a result of this fact. They "first achieved a corporate identity and a name just because they were not parliament."[59]

However, political conditions and the changes which had actually taken place in parliament in the fourteenth and fifteenth centuries meant that this notion of parliament as a court could not long endure without modification. It was clear that, however judicial its functions might appear, parliament was also an assembly of representatives. The sixteenth and early seventeenth centuries saw their further consolidation. New social theories, encouraged by the ideas of the Huguenots and the Presbyterians, made for the increasing political self-consciousness of the house of commons. Representatives, who were no more than "local men, locally-minded, whose business began and ended with the interests of the constituency,"[60] gave way to lawyers and members of the country gentry, who invaded the borough seats. Incited

---

[59] Pickthorn, *Early Tudor Government*, i. 96.
[60] *Interim Report of the Committee on House of Commons Personnel and Politics, 1264-1832* (London, 1932), p. 51.

by the exaggerated claims of the Stuart kings, the commons took issue with the crown directly as to the ultimate basis of authority in the state. The time had come to rationalize the institutions of government in terms of what was to be called popular sovereignty. Yet no real revolution was necessary: people found that what they had come to want to do they had been doing for several centuries. Under royal compulsion they had had much experience and training in self-government. Without knowing what the outcome would be, the English kings had been utilizing to the full the immemorial habits of common action of people in the county, the town, and the parish.

The real basis of what we call institutions must always be in the sentiments of people who operate within their framework: essentially this means the formal and informal organizations of people near the bottom of the social structure. Some coercive authority—objectified in the head of the state— is always necessary as a fiction to give a *sense* of the organization, or to establish "a presumption among individuals in favor of the acceptability of orders from superiors."[61] But authority, in the last analysis, must come from those to whom it applies.

[61] Barnard, *The Functions of the Executive*, p. 170.